THE TRUTH ABOUT LOVE

THE TRUTH ABOUT LOVE

And the lost secrets of true love!

Mark Worthington

First published 2025 by Mark Worthington.

www.mark-worthington.com

Copyright © Mark Worthington 2025

The moral rights of the author have been asserted.

All rights reserved. No part of this book may be reproduced or transmitted by any person or entity, including internet search engines or retailers (including, but not restricted to, Google and Amazon), in any form or by any means, electronic or mechanical, including photocopying (except under the statutory exceptions provisions of the Australian Copyright Act 1968), recording, scanning or by any information storage and retrieval system without the prior written permission of the author.

The author expressly prohibits any entity from using this publication in any manner for purposes of training artificial intelligence (AI) technologies to generate text, including without limitation technologies that are capable of generating works in the same style or genre as this publication. The author reserves all rights to license uses of this work for generative AI training and development of machine learning language models.

Because of the dynamic nature of the internet, any web addresses or links contained in this book may have changed since publication and may no longer be valid. The author of this book does not dispense medical advice or prescribe the use of any technique as a form of treatment for physical, emotional, or medical problems without the advice of a physician, either directly or indirectly. The intent of the author is only to offer information of a general nature to help you in your quest for emotional and spiritual wellbeing. In the event you use any of the information in this book for yourself, which is your constitutional right, the author assumes no responsibility for your actions.

Cover design by Julia Kuris, Designerbility designerbility.com.au

Internal design by Zena Shapter, zenashapter.com

Diagrams and Pictures by Bill Shapter, posbycheckout.com

CONTENTS

INTRODUCTION   9
  What Matters Isn't Matter   9

PROLOGUE   24
  My Relationships with Love   24

PART A: THE NATURE OF LOVE   29
  Chapter 1: What is Love?   30
  Chapter 2: An Analogy for Love   58
  Chapter 3: Your Absolute Connection to Love   61
  Chapter 4: The Critical Importance of Self-Love   75
  Chapter 5: There is No Love in Control   87

PART B: THE ENDLESS HUMAN CYCLE OF SEPARATION BACK TO UNION   101
  Chapter 6: Untold Truths About Separation   102

PART C: HUMAN PARADIGMS OF LOVE   114
  Chapter 7: Popular Paradigms of Love   115
  Chapter 8: The Endless Dance of Masculine and Feminine Energies   128
  Chapter 9: What Happens When the Music Stops?   140

PART D: ADVANCED APPLICATIONS OF LOVE	**157**
Chapter 10: The Power of Conscious Relating	158
Chapter 11: Karmic Lessons of Love	169
PART E: CONCLUDING THIS JOURNEY INTO LOVE	**179**
Chapter 12: Balancing Advice for Masculine and Feminine Counterparts	180
Chapter 13: Remembering Love's Truths	183
Chapter 14: My Ode to Love	189
Chapter 15: Knowing Thyself as Pure Love	191
Acknowledgements	**195**
About the Author	**197**

This book is dedicated to love.

Humanity is obsessed with the concept and feeling of love but, collectively, understands very little about its truths. We dream of true love, yet can't find the winding pathways to its attainment.

We also naïvely cling to the soul mate mythology, even though it causes us much pain, particularly when relationships end unexpectantly. Love itself wants to dispel this myth!

We all desire to love and be loved deep in our hearts, yet we don't really know the full power and intelligence of this pure energy that surrounds us. It has no limits!

Separations and reunions are an important part of life on Earth. Comprehending their true significance, and why they must arise, is the antidote for much suffering.

This book shines a light on the many truths of love that have been sitting in the shadows of ignorance for centuries.
As we evolve as a species, it's important that we understand something that we not only want, but what we truly ARE. Anyone who is on the path to knowing this truth of themselves must start with love, for it is the source of everything in this world. Understand the truth of love and you can unlock the life that your soul knows you are worthy of and wants you to experience.

Who would not want that?

Mark Worthington
Author

INTRODUCTION

What Matters Isn't Matter

Love is What Truly Matters!

Love is so much more than you realise. It is all around us and inside us. It is everywhere. It is everything. It is what we all are at the core. Love is why we are here on this planet – to evolve back to our awareness of its truth – and yet we place so many other things above it, out of ignorance.

Without love, we tend to think we are nothing. The standard dichotomy is that love is either not there, and thus no-thing, or there and everything. Yet it is the source of everything continually! We are always simultaneously nothing yet everything, because love connects us to all there is.

We don't fall in and out of love. We can't, because love is inescapable and always present in our lives. It simply feels amplified in certain circumstances, which triggers our mental belief that love is present. In such situations, love is being dialled up or down by our limiting beliefs.

But regardless of the mask love seems to wear in any given moment, it is *always* acting in our best interests. It can be harsh, and sometimes ruthless, just as it can be intoxicating and joyous – but it is our greatest teacher, and its classroom is inside our hearts. Love teaches, but rarely preaches, for it is patient and eternal.

It speaks to us through our intuition, for it is a force of our truth.

What we don't do enough is listen to its gentle whispers, and choose to learn from it. We wait for it to shout and scream at us before we respond, because we are often deaf to its truths.

No matter what importance we ascribe to it, however, it is all-powerful, eternal, and all-knowing. Thus, nothing else truly matters. We may view it through a keyhole, limiting its breadth; yet it is in everything we see and hold. It is truly the doorway we need to pass through to rediscover our bliss. It will give us what we need, until it gives us what we want, and then more! It has the infinite power to create, though we mistakenly think we can create it!

But love knows us better than we know ourselves, for it is the very essence of us and has wisdom beyond our years. Love is a feeling, and is deeply intertwined with light and consciousness. As we respond to it, it seeks to remind our minds that they are the greatest barriers to these three forces of nature.

These elaborate comments may all sound like a bit of a riddle, but all will be revealed in the following pages.

A Fresh View of Love

All relationships, including romantic ones, can be difficult to master; and, if you're anything like I was, it can be an ongoing challenge in life. Indeed, many of our greatest highs and lows can involve our desire to love and be loved – whether we experience wonderful relationships that stand the test of time, ones that start off good then fall apart unexpectantly, or we are still searching for a particular type of connection.

No matter what you've been through or are going through, a raft of emotions can apply and linger for years, causing us great heartache, as well as feelings of rejection, insecurity and guilt.

Whatever your situation, the prescription for greater happiness in your love life lies within this book. Once you understand the way love truly works, and can dismiss the paradigms of love that you were previously taught, much of the negative emotions that you may have experienced because of disappointments in love can dissolve into the past, leaving you in fresh anticipation of great discoveries and wonderful new possibilities!

Perhaps you have lost faith in love and the opposite sex completely because of past rejections, and you have your walls up? Or you crave self-forgiveness or the strength to forgive a former partner? Or perhaps you are just frustrated with not being able to keep your relationship as mesmerising and beautiful as it was the day you met your partner?

All these experiences and emotions have been a part of my life too. But, as I discovered, there is an opportunity for great peace to descend on your life once you remember the many gifts of love.

Whatever you are going through, this book can help revitalise your faith that the love you always dreamed about is possible for you.

It might take a fresh approach from you or your partner, but that's a small price to pay for the happiness and joy that a more conscious understanding of the truths of love can bring.

The true power of love, and its well-kept secrets, have the potential to change your life and show you how you never did fail in love, you just could not see the bigger 'plot' of your story.

All in life is a choice, and when you live from love in a more conscious way, you have a far greater chance of making better choices, which can take your life to a whole new level.

This may not feel like a light read for some, yet it holds the sparks that can ignite the light within your life, if you let it do so.

Come on this journey into wonder and leave your worries about love behind!

The Bold and Italic Me

Whenever I offer my personal experiences in this book, the words will be shown in bold, italic form.

The Prologue provides more background on my motivations for sharing my understandings of love.

I offer these understandings, not in the guise of a perfect person, for I am far from that, but as someone who has had his own trials and tribulations with love and turned his pain into the power of knowing.

My greatest desire is to share that knowing with you.

Love, Love, Love!

We are all so preoccupied with love, that of course many songs are written in homage to it, or from the despair of its demise. So many stories and movies have love as either the main plot, or a sub-plot.

As you read this book, it is therefore important to acknowledge that popular definitions of love may offer you a great starting point from which to contemplate the true nature of love, but none will be adequate in isolation, because love is so eternal, infinite, ever-present and everywhere.

For example, Virgil, the Roman poet of the Augustus period, famously said that "love conquers all". And who could forget the indelible line sung by Paul McCartney, that "all you need is love." There's also a famous song written by Burt Bacharach called 'What the World Needs Now', and its lyrics are profound – in that the simple answer to 'what the world needs' is love, for everyone.

It does sometimes feel like we're in a world where there is not enough love. Countries are at war, relationships are failing, crime rates are all too high, and happiness is in short supply. Not that this is love's fault, for it is ever-present, infinite, and always seeking to help us make this a better world. We just need to trust it!

Still, none of these attempts at explaining or expressing love will be sufficient, because of the true nature of love.

Our collective naïvety about love's true nature is perhaps most famously depicted in the Nat King Cole song 'When I Fall in Love'. In it, a persona declares their desire to either fall in love completely and forever, or not at all. However, we can't decide how we feel love or to what extent. Falling in love forever can be a myth – a fairytale divorced from both reality and love's true plan for our lives. Love often has a different agenda for us.

The fact is that we live in a universe, and therefore a world, full of love. Love is abundant and infinite in its presence. The only thing stopping it from being dominant in our lives is us, and our illusions about it.

But once we consciously learn to let love live us, rather than us trying to live it, our whole world can shift in so many wonderful ways.

Love is always ready to take our lives to a whole new level. If we let it do so, it will infiltrate and dominate our personal lives, businesses, relationships, health, and interactions with the rest of the universe. Love can lead us forward, we just need to broaden our beliefs about it, and let it become the natural creator of our lives, for that is what it always was and always will be. This is so no matter where we are in our journeys (back) to love.

Indeed, love can feel like our greatest friend one minute, then it can flip and feel like our worst enemy in the next. It can seemingly heal us, then harm us. It can be an utter mystery, because we have lost the ability to see its master plan.

Yet the truth is that love always holds us in its infinite wisdom and tender embrace. Knowing this about love means truly knowing yourself, for love is the core inspiration of all our lives. It is what you and I are, what everyone is, and will define who we will become if we can let it ignite our passions in life.

Love is also the most precious thing that we can offer each other. It is often depicted in many religious paintings and sculptures as flowing out of a golden heart. We all have this energy of love, not just the prophets we revere. All we must do is honour and value our own love, for it is the very essence of who we are, one and all. Love is the eternal flame within you, and it will radiate from within your heart when you get out of the way and let it shine. You can try to give up on love and stop trusting it, but love will never give up on you.

Conversely, when we resist trusting or listening to the love in our hearts, we cut ourselves off from the infinite wisdom of love and rely instead on the rudimentary wisdom of our minds. This can lead to us feeling incomplete, even disconnected from our true authentic selves.

So let us all open ourselves up to the possibilities that love has waiting for us, and explore the principles of romantic love in particular, given it impacts our emotions and sense of well-being so much.

The same principles do apply to other forms of love, but romance is often the hardest form to master.

Love is the Universal Answer

Another understanding that's important to acknowledge as you read this book, is that the power of love is effectively in charge of your life. It can take many years, experiences and deep personal investigation to realise this, but the natural flow of the universe, and therefore our world, is one dedicated to expansion through the power of love.

Love is thus infinitely connected to the creative intelligence of the universe and knows a lot more about you than you know about yourself! Love, with consciousness, manifested every part of your existence, and it brings forth whatever you need to grow your wisdom as it sees fit.

Yes, you have free will, but beware of the consequences of a life lived out of alignment with love. Every step you take away from the true intention of life on Earth, every time you focus on other more temporary things like money or power, you are stepping further away from love, and giving yourself more work in the long run – for eventually love will conspire to bring you home to the truth that you are love, or spirit, living a human life.

That doesn't mean you can't be materially successful in life while living from love. There is nothing wrong with power or money. But when you do what you love, with who you love, to bring love to the world, your chances of being successful are so much higher. Equally, your chances of failing to meet your expectations along the way are far less fragile, and you will enjoy the journey you are on so much more as well. In fact, you might love it!

A big initial question to ask yourself, therefore, is what matters to you most: impressing the world with your external versions of success, loving your life, or experiencing both simultaneously?

Also, how far from your authentic self are you prepared to stray and to what consequences? Sometimes, love's orchestrated diversions back to your heart's desires can be extremely painful and unexpected.

Such were my experiences. Although I did nothing particularly bad in life, I experienced several extremely painful and unexpected disruptions. I could not have foreseen any of them, not from the level of awareness that I was living from at that time, yet I found myself having to weather them anyway, and each one impacted me greatly.

In hindsight, I was essentially oblivious to how and where I was making decisions from in life, and out of ignorance I paid a heavy price, seemingly. I could not see love's master plan, as I was living in my ego and not my heart for many years, and suffered accordingly.

In my earlier years, I even suppressed my heart's desires and went after my version of material success and external validation, out of sheer ignorance that I even had a choice. I was far more intent on impressing the rest of the world than being in love with myself and my own life.

This is so common an approach one might call it normal, but it certainly wasn't and isn't natural.

It was also confusing, since many people who did the same as I managed to sidestep the kind of experiences that befell me. Perhaps their consciousness was higher than mine.

The answer I discovered, from facing my emotional pain, was that in this life, my soul wanted me to expand back to a more loving way of being, and to do so I was being given experiences that were not pleasant to my human self, but which would challenge me to see the truth. I was therefore changing and evolving, and love was the force behind it, for my soul had chosen this path for me, out of love for myself.

Thus, my ego-based decisions and activities were dismantled by the universe one-by-one, because my soul wanted me to become truer to myself.

Now, I'm of course glad that my true self did this for me, for I am much more at peace and excited about my future than ever before.

The key message I learned was that living from the love in your heart ultimately means having a much higher chance of enjoying greater levels of happiness, success, fulfilment and peace, without any unpleasant disruptions.

So, do what you love, love who you really are, make decisions that will bring you joy, speak the truth in your heart, trust that love has your best interests at heart, and learn from all that love teaches you.

Love, love, love – without compromise or regret!

To do otherwise means living with great fragility in your life, for you never know when the forces of love will come calling to play their ruthless cards in the game of your life.

Indeed, just as the universe moves in mysterious ways, so does love – for it is fascinating and divine, but not always kind. It can be harsh when your soul needs it to be, particularly when you ignore the many pleas and inspirations that your heart will regularly send you.

Whereas, when you live in the energy of love with no resistance to what is and what was, the process of evolution will be easier and more fun for your individual self to go through.

Being in the energy of love also gives you a much greater opportunity to choose the life that you want and will love.

Simply put, love is truly living in you, so why not live in alignment with it?

Forgiveness Comes Alive in Love

As you read this book, please know I acknowledge that one of the hardest things for a human being to do is to forgive themselves, or others, when things go wrong or fail to meet their expectations. This is particularly so when it comes to romance.

Indeed, we can often think we have forgiven someone, but the truth is that until we do this through the power of love, our forgiveness is fickle and may not be truly felt.

However, understanding the truth about love gives us the power of forgiveness beyond anything we may have experienced before. When forgiveness comes from our hearts, and not our minds, there is a freedom that we can experience beyond our deepest understandings.

If you have any sadness, hold any grudges or live in regret, I therefore encourage you to absorb the wisdom in this book, for it is truly written for your heart, and for giving you the freedom you deserve to love with passion for the rest of your life.

Moving From Fear to Love

Please note that, essentially, the only way through the psychological and emotional pain arising from our needs not being met is to go through that pain, and not around it.

Negative emotions and thoughts are just energies needing to be put in motion, such that they leave or are replaced by positive energies and beliefs. Every need that is exposed and transcended, brings you closer to your soul energy and allows you to more readily manifest from your heart, not from the lower-based frequencies of separation that reside in your ego.

That said, whenever I mention the concept of 'pain' throughout this book, please note that I am referring to psychological and emotional pain, not necessarily pain that is completely and utterly beyond your personal control, and to which you are not directly contributing, such as pain derived from accidents, conflicts, or diseases. Although a person may have somehow contributed to its existence, medical intervention may be the most potent assistance a sufferer possesses in such instances.

Love is the True Author of Our Lives

Another concept it's important for you to acknowledge as you read this book, is that love is the true author of our lives. In concert with universal energies, it writes the scripts we follow in every chapter of our evolution.

Yet we so often don't trust it, especially if we have experienced great heartache and despair. Many of us lose the art of feeling into it and unknowingly confuse it with its close cousins: attraction and admiration. These two pretenders of love are important, but since they are physical and mental constructs, they are mere surrogates for love.

All three matter in a loving relationship, of course, but one is not the other, and a failure to understand this can lead to relationship breakdowns.

But relationship breakdowns can be good for us, as separation has a deep purpose in our lives – another truth about love that we have forgotten, or not been taught. While we are taught how to think and understand subjects like mathematics and science at school, the subject of how to love is so often neglected as a topic to be understood – is it any wonder that we approach relationships with so much ignorance and naïvety?

Awareness is the way through this mire, yet it is so often covered up by our egoic thoughts and fantasies about relationships.

We also place a huge importance on our loving relationships with others, forgetting that loving ourselves is the most important relationship of all.

Isn't it time we learned to end these important contradictions, by moving from ignorance to higher intelligence when it comes to love.

After all, love is steeped in infinite intelligence. We owe it to ourselves and to future generations to learn to love more fully and consciously.

Our future is dependent upon it.

Love is for ALL

We are all immersed in love. Nature is comprised of love and, therefore, so are we. All of us. There are no exceptions. Which means that this book is for everyone, no matter who they are, or how they identify in this world.

We tend to classify people based on gender and sexuality. But this book does not differentiate in that way, for to do so is steeped in ignorance. Love does not differentiate on this basis, so why would a book about the wisdom of love take this limited perspective?

The truth in this book is welcome to everyone. Love works its magic in our lives through both our soul and sexual energies. Sexuality is beyond human judgement and between you and your soul. The soul chooses its sexuality for its own experience, and whatever people think about that choice is of no relevance at all. This book thus honours and loves you, no matter how you identify yourself. Love invites you into its sacred truths.

Honouring Your Own Love

As you read this book, there is a very powerful principle about love that I hope you choose to take forth into your life. It relates to honouring yourself, for this is where true love can only ever be experienced. And the self I am referring to is your true self, your own heart.

Many of us are so desperate to be loved by those we feel love for, that we dishonour ourselves in the process of trying to love. Our limited awareness of the full spectrum and value of ourselves makes us prone to see ourselves from the perspectives and reflections of the beliefs of others. We tend to act in ways that we think will bring us the love, admiration and appreciation, and in doing so we dishonour, disrespect and cease to accept the wholeness and greatness of ourselves.

When you dishonour yourself, you send an invitation to those around you to dishonour you. That includes your romantic lovers. And love, in its inevitable style, will make sure this invitation is fully accepted, at your expense. It will hold the mirror up to your lack of self-love for deep purpose. That's its job.

When we want to fit in, where we don't truly belong, we will essentially sacrifice our happiness and forget what we deserve. We become like a desperate seagull on the beach begging for scraps. This behaviour is, unfortunately, quite normal in our modern world.

Come on this journey to discover the only way to the true love that you seek. Honour you and you will be honoured in return.

God is the Energy of the Universe

As you read the pages ahead, please note that, while there are many different perceptions of what constitutes God and everyone is entitled to their own opinion in this regard, when I reference God I am referring to the intelligent energy of everything in the universe.

We are all a part of this energetic entirety, which would be diminished if any of our selves ceased to be present, even though this is not possible.

We Are Light Beings

It's also important as you read this book to share my understanding that we are all light beings living a human life, though many of us are generally ignorant to this fact.

We are essentially love-based multidimensional beings who have forgotten this truth, because amnesia of our metaphysical truths is part of the deal we make when we decide to visit Earth in a physical form.

Heaven is thus not a single physical place, as some religions or legends would have us believe. Heaven is the store of our collective light energies, which exists across the whole universe, for it exists wherever love exists, and that is everywhere.

The Complex Relationship Between Love, Light and Consciousness

Continuing on from these understandings, while love has many great powers, it is ultimately related to and grounded within two very powerful forces: light and consciousness. All three are closely intertwined. Love is our doorway to all three forces whilst we are alive on Earth, for our hearts or souls act as our key connection to universal intelligence.

A fundamental understanding of this link is therefore important if you're to understand the true powers of love and the origin of its powers…

Light is an intelligent creative energy of the universe.

Love is a feeling that humans experience that is also infinite and intelligent creative energy expressing itself in this world.

Consciousness is awareness beyond the individualisation of oneself, where one is tapped into the infinite creative energy of the universe.

So, all three are different aspects of the one thing: intelligent, creative energy that is universal and unlimited. All three concepts are words we use to describe the truly indescribable.

Romantic love is a subset of this universal love, being the recognition of the creative universal energy within yourself, which is stimulated by an emotional exchange with another human being. When two human beings recognise this energy within themselves, it can bring forth new life, through the life force that we can express in sexual desire and intimacy.

Living from love allows us to live in alignment with the universe's preferred plan for our existence.

Love is therefore our guide to higher awareness and the truth in our souls. It is the source of great wisdom that can lead us home if we trust it. And trust it we must if we want to evolve as nature intended!

Evolution – the Purpose of Life on Earth

Finally, the last concept I'd like to introduce you to before we begin, is that there are two key purposes of life that we all share: to return to our natural state of pure love as we walk upon the Earth, and by virtue of that to live a life that we love. Simple really!

The word EVOLution aptly includes the word love, spelt backwards. That is not a coincidence, for this is the journey we are all on. We each have different ways of wishing to apply love to, and in, our lives. However, this specific intention or mission can only truly be known or 'evolve' for us when it is felt in the presence of love within us and truly embodied.

The more whole we become, the more alignment we have with the love in our hearts, the purer our intentions to evolve can become, the closer we can get to creating heaven on Earth and returning to love as our primary way of living.

This, however, will require us to evolve back to living in, and making decisions from, our hearts. Essentially, as we purify our thoughts, beliefs and energies, our true loving vibrations can resonate out and manifest into this world.

This is because the universe is not just a huge conglomeration of stars, planets and empty space. It is comprised of pure consciousness or intelligence that manifests into physical and metaphysical energies – and you are it and always were.

As a result, your life is determined by a series of choices made before, and after, you were born. Your soul, which is pure love, is truly behind it all. Your soul has put you here and love is the force behind everything that ultimately happens to you. It even decides when you will die and when you will be reborn. You can resist for a while, but love holds the upper hand and is ever patient, because we are all aspects of God (however you define that), and a part of the oneness of this great universe. We can never truly separate ourselves from this great power, even though we are so often taught that this separation exists. We are in fact pure love, living with the illusion that we are not, and this illusion becomes a delusion in our minds because, for centuries, humanity has told itself that our separation from all else is real, when it is not.

Separation consciousness is the outcome of all this. For centuries human civilisation embraced separation as our truth and was oblivious to the reality that this set of beliefs is a great fallacy, and the core source of much of our suffering.

Humanity did once live in alignment with unity consciousness, with the belief that we are never separate from the rest of the universe, including of course each other. But somewhere along the way we lost this understanding, and our lives plunged into darkness and fear.

So, with all this in perspective, let us now turn our attention to understanding love and how we can fully harness its power in our lives, not the fictitious version of love that we have come to believe in, thanks to popular culture and a lack of education on the truth of love.

PROLOGUE

My Relationships with Love

A Little About Me

It is often said that it's better to have loved and lost, than never to have loved at all. These words hold great wisdom and truths. However, when you are in the grips of another relationship ending, they can feel quite challenging to accept.

They often challenged me too, though I am now so very pleased to be able to use my experiences for your benefit, given they have led me to write this book – not because I was a spectacular success with romantic and other relationships, but frankly, because I wasn't.

As I have described in my other books in more detail, several parts of my life did not meet my hopeful expectations. I lost jobs, got very sick, had two divorces and lost wealth and access to my children commensurate with both. My life was like a rollercoaster of highs and lows, with my relative successes always seemingly succumbing to fragility in the end.

However, all these mishaps made me determined to understand why. Why did this all happen when I tried so hard and stuck to all the rules I had been taught? I was a good boy, so why was I seemingly 'punished' by life so harshly and so often?

I had to find the truth, and for years nothing else mattered to me. My awareness of myself became the new target of my in-built curiosity.

At times I lost my previous passion for 'normal' life but replaced that raw enthusiasm with a need to understand my plight and find my true self amongst the 'ruins'.

I was always a very curious child, and my parents always quipped that I had an annoying desire to understand everything. This curiosity drove me with a burning passion to understand why I had 'failed' so often, when others around me, who were arguably less talented in some ways, had not.

My deep explorations led me to some wonderful self-discoveries that I was totally blind to for most of my life.

Which prompts me to ask you this: would you rather learn from someone who has learned about a subject from a textbook or university course, or someone who has learned from real experiences, imperfections and apparent missteps, then stepped back to see them from a higher level of awareness? I know who I would turn to for advice!

This book is not full of statistics and charts supporting my views. It is backed by the loving force arising from my actual lived experiences and intuition. I urge you to read it with an open heart, for our minds are so often the greatest enemies of accepting new paradigms and truths. And our hearts are the custodians of love, the very subject of this book, my labour of love for you.

My life has been filled with relationships with many wonderful women, all amazing in their own unique ways. But all these relationships ended for one reason or another. Sometimes I ended them and sometimes they did. We all got the gift of learning from these colourful episodes in our lives, and I am eternally grateful that they each chose to spend part of their precious lives with me and helped me to grow through the presence of their love and attention.

I have been divorced twice, which of course no one in their right mind sets out to do. But, ironically, this was my inherent problem for much of my life. My conditioned mind contributed to my demise in romance (and in other walks of my life), not because it did not try to make each romance work (in the ways I thought would best serve my partners and I), but because back then I was not fully conscious of truths about myself or love.

I was essentially flying blind, because no one had ever shown me what it really meant to be in a truly loving and conscious relationship. That's not anyone's fault, because most people are not taught either, so many of us lack the necessary skills and awareness to make our romantic relationships a resounding success!

My sense of failure eventually drove me with a passion to relentlessly understand the truths of love, and my own relationships with it. I know that this is not normal, but I could not resist my desire to really know myself intimately.

I had been conditioned to understand relationships from what I had witnessed growing up, either from watching my parents interact, the media, movies or other relationships I had observed. My limiting beliefs had essentially set me up to taste a lack of success. But I own this and do not blame others, for I chose it all.

But the reality is that I never failed as such, not because the relationships stood the test of time, but because later in my life I took the time, alone, and with some incredibly wise mentors, to gain higher understandings from the pain I had endured. This then turned those failures into success!

This is actually a core component of any journey to higher self-awareness, to learn from joy and pain – although pain often gives us a greater incentive to grow than joy. Mine certainly did, and ended up becoming the fuel for my own transformation.

I'm not a trained psychologist with a degree in that specialisation, but I have gained a degree from the university of life, and it was a degree that cost me a lot more than university fees! Essentially, I paid a high price for great learnings each time a romance ended in the pain of loss and disruption.

And part of my learnings truly came from the universe as I sought wisdom from all avenues available to me. I was desperate to understand *why some people seemed to be able to sustain loving relationships on a long-term basis, when other people seemingly could not get it right. Was it luck, was it skill, was it divine intervention?*

After ten years of extensive research that connected me to the wisdom of psychologists, life coaches, great scriptures, philosophers and metaphysical mentors beyond this world, I arrived at a higher level of awareness about the intent of loving relationships and why some work and some don't. I finally understood the essentials of love and life.

This wisdom is now very precious to me, and I trust it will be a 'superpower' in all future love adventures that I choose to enter!

It could be for you too. In fact, I would love this book to help anyone starting out on a romantic endeavour, or anyone who's lost trust in love, to understand that all relationships are experiments offering us a loving mirror capable of shining a light on our own limiting beliefs and energies. This took me so many years to understand!

But once I forgave myself for my trail of missteps, I finally found peace in acceptance. I accepted all that was, and all that is, in my love journey, to allow myself to trust what would and could possibly be. And this acceptance was built on the foundation of finally understanding love and how it operates.

Self-forgiveness was a crucial first step. It may be easy for some people to achieve, but for most people who have had multiple disappointments like I did, it can be a great challenge, given how much failed romances can hurt. The hurt can affect so many other parts of your life too, such as your wealth, family structure, access to friends, and even your reputation in the eyes of others. Its impacts can reach far and wide.

But forgiving yourself and others for what took place is easier once you learn to look at life through the prism of love.

Love is the answer to so many of our unsolved mysteries. It holds the key to our happiness, and in its most raw of powers it can create new people.

Love is the great healer of so many things. Its power is immense.

It's time we listened to love's words of wisdom for it is a huge force in our lives, and one we truly cannot control. We can never own it.

Not everyone wants to welcome truths into their lives, of course, for many people are content to stay at their current level of awareness.

This was never me, and I trust if you are reading this book, that it is not you.

PART A

THE NATURE OF LOVE

CHAPTER 1

What is Love?

Natural Truths of Love

There is so much that this book will share with you about love, its purpose and nature. But first, let us consider your starting point – when it comes to normal paradigms of love, the following statements are likely to represent very familiar concept to readers. However, as you progress throughout this book, I encourage you to understand the natural truths of love, which the following table reveals:

Normal Paradigms of Love	Natural Truths of Love
"Love is wonderful!"	Love is a teacher of truth, and can therefore be ruthless and brutal, as well as beautiful.
"I am so ready for love!"	Only your heart knows when you are truly ready for love.
"Attraction is a big part of who I fall in love with."	Love and attraction are separate. Attraction is a mental / physical construct. Love is metaphysical.
"I think I'm in love!"	Love is beyond thinking. It can only ever be felt.

"Our love will last forever!"	The only love you can rely upon forever is your own self-love. Romances are experiments designed to teach us, and as such may not last. Many of them must end so the next one can begin.
"I need to be in a relationship to feel complete."	Love 'punishes' need but supports want and desire.
"I hate being alone!"	Separation is part of the human experience. Its pain helps us to discover more about ourselves.
"It's all your fault!"	Relationship issues are no one's fault – they're love's way of holding a mirror up to our conditioned beliefs, helping us to grow.
"I need to try harder to foster love in my relationships."	Love cannot be controlled or created. It is bestowed upon us and controls us. Surrendering to love and letting it find the way forward is our natural way to live.
"This time, I'm waiting for true love!"	All love is true. We are not, because our egos are usually not.
"I'm very picky about who I love."	Romantic love is a vibrational or frequency match. As such, you cannot pick it. There is love between ALL human beings.

"When will I find my soul mate?"	We all have many soul mates, but only one twin flame. The belief that soul mate love is the ultimate form of love is a myth.
"I hate it when love dies."	Love never dies, we just sometimes move out of a frequency match with others, in order to find a better frequency match.
"I can't wait for love to come along again!"	Love is always here, because all human beings are pure love at their core. It is ever-present in all of us. Open to it, for love is waiting for your invitation to grace your path unencumbered.
"I hope that, when I find love again, it will…"	Love doesn't care about our expectations or hopes. It just is what it is.
"That song describes love so perfectly!"	Love is indescribable. Even the word love is insufficient to do it justice.
"Time heals all wounds."	Love is the true healer, not time.
"I don't think I'll ever forgive them."	You cannot think forgiveness; it can only ever come from the heart and be felt.
"It was love at first sight!"	Yes, but love is found in the eyes, not in the body. Eyes are the windows to our souls.

"They make me feel so loved."	You can only ever feel your own love. Your partner's words and actions can stimulate your own heart. But, ultimately, it's your level of self-love that decides how loved you feel.
"Love is such a great feeling!"	Love is a powerful creative source, for it is grounded in pure intelligence or consciousness. But yes, it can feel great.
"Love is all we need!"	Yes, it can be all we need; but we also live in a physical world and therefore attraction and admiration matter too. The best relationships are grounded in both love and attraction.
"Our love is tainted now."	Love is always pure. It can, however, be tarnished by our egoic needs, attachments and fears. Some of these may be generated by the life circumstances we are experiencing in this incarnation, and some may be karmic and relate to past lives.
"You never know when love will happen!"	Love can arrange relationships using karmic and soul-based contracts, and some of these are predetermined by our souls and the souls of others before we are born. Love will most likely arise when you least expect it.

"Love never works for me."	The practice of 'conscious relating' allows love to create the relationships that we truly desire and need. Love creates such infinite possibilities through feelings and truth.

Let's now look at a few explanations about love, which will assist as you read on.

Love is a Frequency, Not a Noun or Verb!

The word love is one of the most used words in the English language or vernacular, and yet it truly is impossible to find a way of describing it completely or fully. I challenge you to do so!

Perhaps this is because love is a feeling and cannot be thought. It just is and cannot be created by our minds. It is beyond our normal concepts. Just consider the number of times the word 'love' has and will feature in this book – how could it not, for it is difficult to describe in any other way. I don't apologise for its repetition. I marvel at its significance, for love lies at the core of us all.

We are all pure love, although this is a concept that humanity has largely forgotten in its quest to be loved.

Ironic, isn't it? We chase what we already have and already are. We have forgotten that we are essentially a frequency. We think we are solid physical beings with a brain. Thus our metaphysical truths remain a mystery to most, shrouded by our long-held conditioned mindsets.

But the love in each of our hearts vibrates at a frequency that is unique to each of us and, in a sense, we are all like large tuning forks vibrating at our own pitch. As a result, we resonate with some people and experiences, and not with others.

So, how does that *resonate* with you right now? Before we go on, can you at least accept that all in this universe, and therefore by default our world, is energy – an electromagnetic field – and that at the core of this field is love?

Can you then also accept that you are energy too, and thus love? Can you accept that love is the generator of you, that your energy field, body, mind and soul determine your collective energies, and as such you have your own frequency or pitch?

Because it's true! All energy has its own different frequency that ultimately defines it, for all is light in one sense or another. The way something looks, the way it feels and how we respond to it, is then all down to the frequency of our own individual energy, and how we interact with other energies. Further, we often attract the same energy that we put out.

Our energy frequency determines our lives and whether we need to be in different paradigms of union or separation at any point, i.e. in or out of a romantic relationship.

Our frequency also determines how we feel and how we express ourselves in this world. Our thoughts are no match for such energetic realities and will always be overcome in the end by our vibrational pitch.

Your vibration is everything, for it is your level of resonance with love. Lost resonance with your true frequency is thus a lost opportunity for bliss, and to love your life.

If you can rediscover your way home to the loving relationships that your heart desires, including your relationship with yourself, then you can finally let love write your story, and shine through you with grace.

Love being a frequency also explains why we love music so much, and why some music resonates for some and not others – it's in line with our own vibrational pitch and reinforces our own internal frequency – and why sometimes we feel like listening to a certain song and sometimes we don't.

Essentially, both our bodies and music are waves of light, interacting with each other. And perhaps this is why so many songs are written about love, for they are love like us.

In Bruce Johnston's song 'I Write the Songs', made famous by Barry Manilow, he voices this very connection between music and love, the lyrics telling us that love is the source of music. Perhaps that's why so much love is expressed through song? You be the judge!

I doubt many have heard the lyrics of this song in their full power, because they are beyond our collective perceptions of the relationship between love, and music.

So why do we feel love for some people and not others?

This may sound a bit too scientific, and not romantic enough for some readers, but the truth is that when we meet someone who is a close or exact frequency match with our own vibration, we feel love for that person or experience, because we are resonating with each other.

Mix that frequency match with attraction (which we will address below), and boom a relationship explodes in the petri dish of love.

I use this analogy with respect to relationships, since a petri dish is commonly used in laboratory experiments, and all relationships are experiments. They allow us to remember the love that we are on the inside. That's the point of any experiment we experience in love.

When we meet others, we can thus connect with them on different levels – including mental and physical levels, or in our soul energy on a metaphysical or spiritual level.

Love is felt in our bodies, for it is a feeling, and a pure vibration. It is, however, beyond our mental control as human beings, as it resonates metaphysically.

Attraction is Not Love

Attraction involves a combination of lust and compatibility, with lust being a sexual or physical connection and compatibility being a mental connection or preference. It is largely perceived by the mind and its propensity to be conditioned to certain needs and wants. Some may refer to attraction as admiration. They are highly correlated.

Love and attraction can matter to people in differing degrees, depending on whether they are primarily living from their egos, or their soul energy. In romantic relationships they both matter, though one is more controllable than the other.

I have heard it said that admiration is necessary before love can be present. However, this is not true. Love is completely beyond our control and is distinct from mental constructs. There is no love in control and mental control can never establish love.

Many people also confuse love and attraction. And, when love gets lost in the burning fire of attraction, romantic relationships can feel fickle and temporary. But love itself can never die – it is of a high purity and uncorrupted by thought. When a relationship ends, and we say we have lost love for another, what is happening is that we're moving out of our previous vibrational match with someone.

Love can, however, be overridden by the human ego, because the human mind can incorrectly believe that it is the source of love. This can never be and is an illusion that humanity experiences on a grand scale. The human mind and body can express the feelings of love that arise within our hearts and are felt in our bodies, but this expression is not love and never can be. It's just the messenger.

Attraction to others is still very important of course, particularly lust, for we do live in a dense physical environment on Earth, and are programmed to promulgate the species by creating children. Making love is one of the most extraordinary experiences available to us all!

But, when we confuse love with attraction, we can enter relationships with one of the key ingrediencies that we deeply desire in short supply, and we may not realise this until we have already made promises to another.

Love, on the other hand, is so spectacular that it can engulf our senses, like a sunrise or sunset. I might describe a sunset to you, but they would just be words. They are not the sunrise or sunset itself.

In the same way, a sense of love that is only thought, and not a close frequency match, is more likely to be attraction, and thus temporary in its magnetism, for it lives in the illusion of personal preferences and choices, and is subject to fluctuations in our conditioned mindsets.

We can still feel attraction within us, but it is a message felt in our bodies that originates from the physical aspects of ourselves, not from our hearts. Accordingly, when we meet people, it is valuable to feel into the energy of attraction that we are experiencing, before we think about it. Perhaps there is something about them that intrigues us and would add to our lives in a positive way, yet it doesn't meet the normal constructs of our mindsets. Is there joy to be found in such a union? If so, we may benefit from embracing this opportunity.

Love may still be present between the two souls, but it might not be strong enough to withstand those same fluctuations. How magnetic the love is between two souls, and how strong the frequency match is, will determine the relationship's length, and we can't think the answers, we just receive them from our hearts. And that's the trick that often fools us.

Attraction can fade over time, or in an instant in the face of a particular event, as can admiration. So, if our feelings are swamped by a loss of attraction, or perhaps usurped by a higher vibrational match, perhaps it wasn't the purity of love that our hearts were seeking in the first place.

We may be sexually attracted to a person, and then their body shape changes because of a particular event, which can change our level of attraction and may even impact our compatibility; but our metaphysical love won't necessarily fade, because our hearts don't and can't stop loving other hearts. Love itself will only be affected if the vibrational pitch of the other person's frequency also changes. In that case, love can become less appealing, or may even be replaced by the love for another who becomes a closer frequency match.

If one person in a relationship does the inner work to shift their vibrational frequency, a relationship can break. It may feel like love has died, but the reality is that the match has shifted somehow.

I've been 'left' by partners who said they loved me, often for years, but at some point wanted to pursue a stronger vibrational match. That was not easy to accept, but it's love's way of altering our physical realities for a purpose.

This is why 'conscious relating' within a romantic relationship is so critical if we want it to last and grow in intensity. 'Conscious relating' is a method of communicating with your partner wherein you both enter interactions with the intention of helping each other to learn and grow. It involves being fully self-aware of your thoughts, feelings and behaviours, willing to express these and empathise with your partner's, being mindful of each other's vulnerability, and committed to your mutual and personal evolution. We will explore conscious relating further throughout the book, and particularly in Chapter 10.

Essentially, however, if we don't grow within a relationship, love will let us know, because to evolve fully we need to let love build our relationships with others. And if two people in love do not evolve their awareness levels together, vibrational differences can easily arise, disturbing the frequency match we call romantic love, either temporarily or permanently, resulting in a perception that we have grown apart or fallen out of love. What has grown apart is their respective vibrations, their essences of love or the truths within their hearts.

Love is Always Pure, Our Minds Are Not

There is no other form of love than pure love, and this is always true.

The distorted conditioning of our minds and other karmic energies can get in the way of love being given and received, and the frequency of the love that we are can also vary depending on our own personal vibrations, but that doesn't change love's core purity.

Imagine the different sounds generated by a violin or a piano. Both create different sounds at different vibrations, but the sounds given off by both are pure if they are properly tuned. This is an analogy for love. We are all like musical instruments with our own unique pitch.

But our minds and energies determine how pure we resonate with the other instruments around us. If a whole orchestra is using instruments that are out of tune, the performance they give will lack in finesse – the audience and the conductor will certainly *not* love it!

Our world at times can feel like this – a bit chaotic. But the more we retune ourselves, by purifying our egos and coming home to higher awareness of self, the purer our love can feel within ourselves and with the outside world.

Why and How Do I 'Feel' Love?

The truth of love is all about YOU. When you meet someone with the same frequency, we call this love, and we ascribe that love to be an energy emanating from another.

One heart feels a burst of joy, and so does the other heart, for they have been reminded of the love that they craved to remember.

Physical distance between two hearts is not relevant, for love is metaphysical and is therefore felt through the ether over any distance. This is why you can feel love for another person, no matter where they are on the planet.

Even in death love endures, because our souls do not cease to exist in death, they just become fully present in other dimensions. Souls can communicate across dimensions for they are multidimensional and omnipresent.

When you meet someone at the same frequency as you, they allow you to connect more fully with the love in your own heart.

We don't like to think of love this way because it goes against the normal way we perceive it. We think we are feeling the other person's love. But we are not! When we meet another at the same frequency as ourselves, their vibration essentially helps to fill the void we *thought* existed in our own hearts, whereas we are simply connecting with the love we already are, stimulating self-love.

We often refer to humans having a broken heart or a hole in their hearts, but this is a fallacy because our hearts are already whole. The barriers to our own frequency may be diminished temporarily, or over a longer period, depending on the relationship circumstances. Our minds may also believe in the illusion of separation, and their limiting beliefs can lead us to feel incomplete or unlovable. But the key to feeling complete is to live in a constant state of frequency alignment, which is why so many feel a constant need to be loved by another person, and why the underlying lack or self-love that they were already experiencing is exposed when that love or vibration is taken away.

The same is not necessarily true, however, when two lovers meet who are already fully in love with themselves, and who have found the purity of their true selves. In this magical place, both individuals are already in the energy of pure uninterrupted love within themselves, and in this frequency the full truth of love is felt without any resistance or consequence should those lovers then part. But this is extremely rare.

In this case, the love within both hearts' overflows onto the other without any need, creating a magical experience few get to feel, until they reach this vaulted place. This state of mutually shared unconditional love is what we normally call true love.

The exciting thing about how this aspect of love works is that you don't need a partner to feel totally loved, because it's your own vibration of love that determines the level of love that you can receive. So, love yourself completely first, then you'll be capable of aligning with the energy of your true loving match when they do come along.

That said, regardless of your relationship status, you can always be in the energy of true love, if you are your true self.

The Purity of Love

The strength of love that two lovers might feel is impacted by its perceived purity, which is the product of two key factors:

- The inherent matched frequencies of the two lovers, and

- The level of disturbance that the lovers experience in their lives, created by their mental constructs, preferences, and personal circumstances, and/or karmic energies.

Making a romantic relationship wonderful can be complex because so many factors can be at play, and many of these can be subconscious to us. Sometimes love gets drowned out by many of these forms of interference. Despite its best efforts, it may not be able to penetrate the many obstacles that we put in its way, particularly if we are oblivious to its presence, and how precious it really is.

The diagram below illustrates this pictorially:

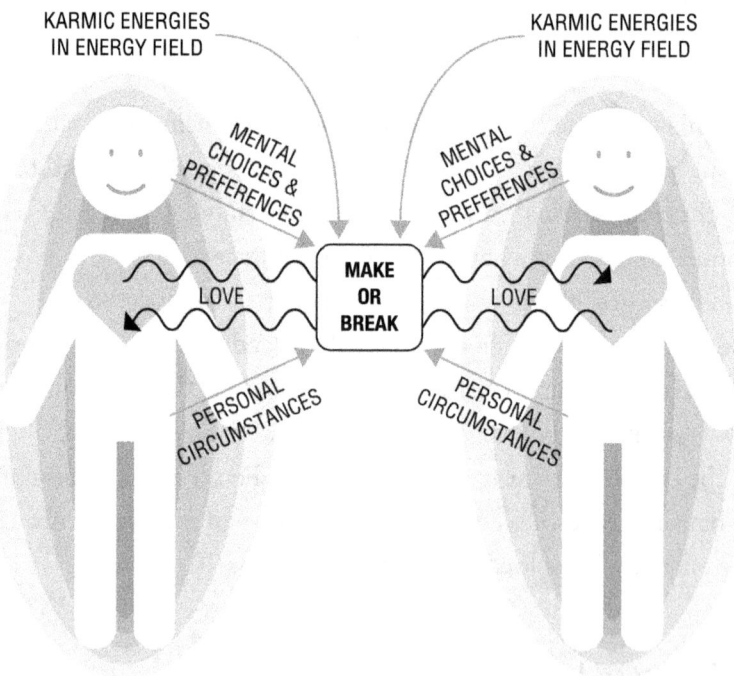

Figure 1: The Complexity of Romantic Relationships

The way we perceive love can be akin to listening to a radio. All the stations are at different levels of frequency, but the level of interference present can be phenomenal, and can directly determine how well we feel the signal. Our souls create the vibration, and our minds and karma create the static and reduce love's perceived purity. Just look at how much static can get in the way of love! Unless we can clear or reduce the interference, how will another heart ever resonate with the love you have in your own?

Throughout this book, we will look at ways to reduce the static and increase your chances at love. It starts with understanding what we're trying to make clearer to others, which is the natural vibrational pitch of our hearts, as determined by our soul's dimensional positioning within the universe.

There are 12 dimensions in the universe at present, and the number of dimensions that exist will continue to expand into eternity. Like a modern corporation with a hierarchy, our true selves can also continue to expand as our souls enrich themselves, with different experiences that bring higher levels of awareness and frequencies to our soul's eternal journey. We continue to progress up through these dimensions as eternity unfolds. It is not a race, for there is no finish line or destination, the universe just keeps adding to its suite of dimensions as evolution unfolds. It is infinite and will always expand.

The higher our dimensional frequencies go, the more intense the love that we experience, though the 'harder' it may also be to meet a frequency match – theoretically. Our souls don't actually care about mathematics and the laws of probability. They know who our right matches are, well before our personalities do, so it's not something we should worry about. Synchronicities will always go hand in hand with the matching process. We just need to open to love and let it find our right matches. You might say, God's got this, you don't need to worry. Just wonder who will come into your life next. How liberating is that!

On Earth we all live in a condition known as duality. We can live from our egos (or personalities) or from our soul energies. Some call this living from the mind or the heart. The choice is ours, although many do not realise that these two separate operating systems are available within them. You are essentially like a computer with different software at your disposal.

This choice is discussed in greater detail in my book *Where Your Happiness Hides*.

Historically, life on Earth has also entailed us living under the influence of our own karma. With each life we tend to accumulate karmic energies, associated with the experiences we chose in our incarnations. Some souls have manifested many incarnations on Earth and carry much karma, whereas some souls have lived very few lives on this planet, or perhaps only one, choosing to be present in other galaxies and dimensions for the bulk of their eternal lives thus far.

Our egos are the product of our conditioning in this life and the remnants of our conditioning from what we call past lives. Both impact our frequency as we walk the Earth.

Karma is discussed later in this book in more detail, for it impacts our ability to connect to our hearts, limiting our ability to embody our true frequency of love. Some might call this spiritual mumbo-jumbo, but this book is about truth and both egoic and karmic energies can severely overwhelm the deep loving soul connection or frequency that one human being may feel with another.

For example, you may fall in love with someone but stop yourself from expressing or even surrendering to that love, because you are not attracted to some aspect of them, such as their personality, age, race, religion, looks or career success. It can get quite complex for there are multiple factors at play. Thus the love may be of a high vibration, but the level of corruption emanating from your thoughts and fears, for whatever reason, are less than ideal to allow the love to flourish fully in its potential level of purity.

Rather than allowing love to create what is possible between two lovers and working on the acceptance of the differences, the mind and our karmic fields can, and so often does, override the situation and derail what was possible, or even intended.

Some things may be inescapable barriers to a loving relationship depending on your perspectives. Examples could be age gaps or physical distance between the lovers.

I had two relationships with women who were a fair bit younger than me. One cared about the age gap, but the other didn't care at all. I pass no judgement, for both perspectives were valid.

Two lovers may also meet, but they are not ready to be together yet, as one or more of the parties need to remove some density of thought or energy that is stopping the frequency match from being in its fullness. Perhaps they will come together at a later point and perhaps they won't. All is a choice.

Our egos protect and project us in all walks of life, unless they are healthy. This is the ego's assumed but illusory role and can impact heavily on our romantic relationships.

When our egos and karmic wounds are diminished, we can surrender more fully to the vibration of love that is the essence of us.

One wonders how much love can and will be felt in romantic relationships across the world when we learn to surrender to love and allow it to 'paint' the depth of our romantic relationships with its colourful wisdom, rather than people mentally judging what level of love is present, and getting it confused with attraction.

You can't think love – learn to feel into it instead.

The Harsh Face of Love

Despite being inherent in the core of what we are, love can seem incredibly cruel and unfair. Just consider all the bad things that happen in this world every day. This can confuse many people, particularly those who worship a god, because it appears to introduce a contradiction into their faith. If God is all-loving, why do bad and sad things happen? Why does God let people die cruel deaths or suffer from diseases?

The explanation lies in the truth of love. We think of love normally in soft and fluffy terms, and see it wrapped in hearts and bows. But love wears different faces, some pleasant and joyous, and some that appear to be harsh and ruthless.

Why is this so?

Well, as I said above, we are all here to evolve back to love. Therefore, the Earth is a place of both joy and learning – some might say remembering not learning, for there is truly nothing we can teach our souls.

Love is everywhere and always on our side, giving us what we need before it gives us what we want.

But what we need to experience to grow our awareness and advance the vibration of our souls will not always feel positive. In fact, it may even feel cruel or even result in our human death.

Unfortunately, humans normally learn better from pain than from joy, and love, in its infinite wisdom, knows this. This makes sense because what we generally enjoy we tend to want to keep doing more of. But when we feel pain, we are often propelled to change, to protect ourselves from the same experience being encountered again.

A more advanced understanding of love requires us to comprehend that life is living us, we are not living it. Essentially our souls are having this experience on Earth for their own benefit, not the separate personality or entity that lives by your name.

Because life is living you, you are not living it. Let that sink in!

Love doesn't want your personality to suffer, but sometimes it must for your wholeness to grow, as intended by your soul. What you resist will persist! When you resist love, it will thus persist in encouraging you to grow into your awareness and levels of love.

It can be hard on your human being, of course, but what you are experiencing in life is taking place for purpose. Nothing is random. The universe does not make mistakes, for it is infinite in its intelligence. And everything is taking place for the good of the whole universe, for we are all a part of universal consciousness.

When we live from our minds, and not our hearts, we are living from our limited intellects. The universe operates from infinite intelligence, and herein lies a distinct misalignment until we choose to address it. And love's intelligent agenda is to create this alignment as we evolve.

While people are programmed to believe that they are separate from all else, this is an illusory mindset called separation consciousness. The reality is that we exist in total connection to all things, known as unity consciousness. The universe is basically just a big experiment with souls working on their awareness levels, like a big university of life. And each time we graduate, our souls go to a higher vibration or dimension.

Earth, however, is where souls can learn to love in a dense environment. In some parts of the universe beings exist in pure light, but here they exist in physical form, and whether we're aware of this or not, we are here to eliminate our karmic energies and negative beliefs. That's the experiment in which our souls have chosen to take part. Our hearts can then step in and take our lives to a whole new level, guided by the divine force of love, for you are it.

To do this though, we need to experience difficulties and learn from them. That's the truth of life on Earth. It can be a harsh experience but will be less so when we return to our true state of being and accept that we are here to learn and love.

Another phase used to describe this state is that of the true self.

From a soul perspective we are eternal beings, and our souls are ambivalent as to whether we have a hard time or a good time while we're here. It would prefer not to see you, the personality it has manifested, suffer, but ultimately the choice is yours, like everything in life.

If we believe in suffering and fear it – guess what we will experience, under the law of vibrational attraction? You get what you put out!

You can either learn to grow closer to the love in your heart, or continue to resist and open yourself up to the consequences of your choices – which will likely involve living with a limiting attachment, fear or belief that does not serve your path to higher conscious awareness, which your soul was trying to get you to change. You dishonour yourself, and attract into your life energies that reflect that, which will in turn further dishonour you.

How are you honouring yourself in your life and your relationships? This is a powerful question we can all ask ourselves regularly as we go through life. Your answers can enshrine great possibilities for you to continually evolve.

But if you learn a lesson and embody its wisdom, it is unlikely to repeat again in this life, for you will have transcended the painful experience the soul wanted you to endure on its behalf. Everything that happens in life happens for and through you, not to you, for it is orchestrated by your soul. Its intent is always to bring you into wholeness, where your mind, body and spirit are in sync.

While love may therefore appear to have different faces, depending on the mask that you think you see – it does only have one face, and it's all love, a naturally kind, compassionate, caring, composed, patient and non-judgemental love that thrives in the innocence of what psychologists call your inner child.

Love does not care about time, because it works off the coalescing of energy, so you may get what you need when you least expect it, but all will be due to love – the good and the bad.

Indeed, few humans blame the bad events that befall them on love, because this is not conventional thinking. The ego-centric mind will typically seek to blame other people or other forces for its misadventures, preferring to deflect attention away from the possibility for deep and important learning. Or we might sometimes blame a misadventure on what we call bad luck, but this too is a misnomer. Everything in life happens for a reason. Accordingly, blaming bad luck merely defers the opportunity for growth.

If we can accept that love is behind it all, we can free ourselves from seeing bad experiences as disasters. Sure, they may be brutal on those involved, but when problems strike we can learn to see them as learning opportunities. Here we come into alignment with the truth. Our awareness is being given the chance to be upgraded. Once we learn to process this pain, and even love its messages, we can take our lives to a higher level.

Love is Ever-Present

We are all connected to one another by love. All souls love each other, with no exceptions, for we are all a part of the universal field of light, consciousness, and love.

We generally only refer to love being present where there is a close frequency match, or when family constructs are in place. However, love is ever-present with all. We just need to open our awareness to it and let it be felt.

Unfortunately, our egos constantly limit the feelings of love that we are prepared to surrender to with other human beings. Our egos have a limited perception of love and block its widespread recognition, preferring to believe that love can only take certain forms or shapes.

Families can change shapes over time, but the truth is that the love between family members and ex-lovers never goes away. It can't, because it is ever-present. It can, however, be altered in its purity and alignment as we change our mindsets and energies, responding to situations and individual neediness for validation.

But since love is ever-present and always on the side of evolution, why not surrender to its omnipresence, now you know that you can?

Love Knows No Barriers

Love is infinite, for it is grounded in infinite intelligence. It sees no limits or barriers.

Only our minds create barriers.

So, if you allow love to take you on its merry ride through life, it can and will show you your true path, and it will never give up, regardless of the circumstances. As infinite intelligence, it will always find a way forward to what is intended. It doesn't care about borders, nationalities or religions. It shines through all barriers that our human minds want to put in the way. We just have to get out of the way of its infinite wisdom.

One day the world will understand that our resistance to love is futile and not in our interests. We will become so much more together if we love in harmony.

But for now, all we can do is develop our awareness about the barriers our minds are creating for us, which we can overcome if we surrender to the truth.

How Do I Create Love with Another Person?

A strong frequency match with another soul is something that is bestowed upon you by the universe. It either is, or isn't! Your personality cannot create this for you, for your mind and body are not consciousness – they are temporary manifestations of consciousness. Your soul knows which souls in this world have a frequency that aligns with yours, as do those matching souls. So, you cannot create love with another person, your mind cannot even detect when you meet a soul mate. But your soul knows.

All you can do is ensure your soul energy becomes the dominant energy within your being, so you can come into higher levels of awareness of when these energy exchanges occur.

My book *From Pain to Possibility* explains a natural way to this state of being, should a reader seek to understand it. However, for the most part this is not common, even though it is possible for us all.

We prefer to do what we are programmed to do as human beings when we want to create love with another person – we go out on dates, have intimate physical experiences, and perhaps engage in emotional conversations.

But this thinking is false and is driven by conditioned mindsets. Shared activities can enhance attraction of course, confirming or denying that we have physical, emotional or mental compatibility with another. But attraction is not love.

Love is usually found in the eyes, as the eyes are the window to the soul. A deep gaze into another's eyes will naturally tell you if love is present. You will feel it in your heart, and it is unmistakeable. I'm sure many readers have had this experience.

When we meet someone with a close frequency match, we will often feel it in our whole being. We can be drawn to their energy, before we have even met them or spoken to them. The souls have connected, and you feel compelled to meet them. You don't need a date to feel this!

Indeed, try as hard as you like, but if a close frequency match is not present, it simply won't arise, unless and until the respective frequencies of two individuals can perhaps come together through inner work, developing awareness, or perhaps through the practising of conscious relating.

As a person lifts or drops their vibration, the suite of people that they can be a vibrational match with can also alter. A very high vibrational person is likely to have less vibrational matches than a person at more normal vibrational levels. But you only need one, and your soul knows where and how to find them.

So you don't need to seek love, because the love you seek is also seeking you. Trust in love and love will find you!

Even then, when we 'fall in love' with another soul we are essentially remembering or discovering the resonance our souls already share. We are not 'creating' love. Love creates itself and does not need our help.

By spending time together, we may also stimulate our own self-love, by essentially thinking to ourselves, 'wow, this person and I are great together, and they love me so I must be amazing too'. Endorphins kick in and we are hooked on our own perception of love. But what happens if the other person's interest in you diminishes and you spend less time together? That's generally when you discover that your own self-love needs more work.

People do often speak of love at first sight. This is possible, if deep eye contact is made in that version of first sight. But love will not be established by staring at a person's body or sharing an email conversation, unless the two souls remember each other through the ether. The souls must energetically connect, and energy needs to be shared for love to be known.

You might feel a resonance with another, by being in their presence, but this must be felt. You won't find a soul connection by thinking it into reality.

In these modern times, where so much communication occurs through texts and email and other forms of social media, we are unfortunately limiting how much presence we are opening ourselves up to on a regular basis.

Feeling Into Love Fast With Your Heart as a Geiger Counter

Entering a loving relationship can be like parking a car. You can go in forward and fast, but you may need to back out later, and this can be a slow and difficult process.

Alternatively, you can take your time and back your car into the car space gradually, doing the hard yards early on. This makes it easier to get out fast, because you have been patient and taken the time to do the hard bits.

It's the same with relationships. Drive in forwards to assess love. But when you are assessing compatibility, maybe back in instead.

Twice in my life I have felt deep love with women without dating them or even a word being spoken. All it took was a brief interlude and a penetrating look into their eyes.

Logic and thought did not have time to even intervene. The souls connected and a kind of remembering had surely taken place.

Both experiences reverberated through my body, and I was hooked.

But I didn't take enough time to determine if sufficient attraction was present. This caused me much pain down the track, when both women decided I wasn't for them, because their polarity with me was insufficient for them.

Call it a rookie error, made by a man with limited dating expertise!

Determining whether a sufficient frequency match is present, is a feeling exercise. You need to connect to your heart and allow it to tell you if love is there.

I had to learn to do this in a meditation state, so that I could take my logical mind out of the equation.

But some of us aren't good at this for we have not been taught to feel, and the logical mind seems far more equipped to assess attraction and compatibility.

In my life, I have had several relationships where I was compatible with some wonderful women. What ended each of these relationships, however, was truth. It was only once I stopped thinking about compatibility and attraction and accessed the truth in my heart that I was able to discern whether a strong enough frequency alignment, capable of being called pure love, was present.

These days I do this deep soul-searching at the very beginning of a new relationship or chance meeting to determine if the relationship is based on a close enough sense of love.

If it's not present, I now end the relationships quickly or not enter them at all, because a strong feeling of love is a non-negotiable in all my romantic relationships.

I carry my heart around as a kind of Geiger-counter, as crazy as that may sound!

Have you ever persevered in a romantic relationship and hoped that, with the passing of time, it would lead you to a strong sense of love, but then frustratingly it didn't?

Hope is a controlling energy, originating in the mind, and one that the universe does not respond to positively. It responds to trust and surrender. It knows who you are meant to date or be with next, according to your divine life plan.

Trust your heart, for it is connected to the all-knowing universe, and a close frequency match will be yours when you simply surrender to the infinite intelligence of your soul.

Because love is a feeling, not a thought, it is also impossible for other people to advise us on what is truly at play in a relationship. You must trust your own heart and feel for the presence of deep love. No other heart can feel into it for you. So, forget matchmakers and well-intending friends and relatives telling you who you should love. Let your feelings fulfil that role for you.

Just live your life with passion and let your soul provide the colours of life that you need to experience next.

The dating scene is a bit like an ice cream parlour. There are many different flavours for you to experience, but only your heart, communicating through your body, knows which flavours you are meant to love and embrace in any given moment.

You may need to explore a few flavours to know which ones suit you best!

Remember, your heart does not lie!

The Winding Path to the Love We Seek

We all dream about true love. We want nothing more than to love and be loved with the full force of our hearts, and by the hearts of others.

True love is etched into our psyche and is constantly referred to – unfortunately somewhat naïvely. The truth is that true love is possible for all. Though rare and hard to come by, there is a natural path to true love. But no short cuts!

Many couples believe they have found true love, only to have their illusions smashed upon the rocks that their egos assembled.

Read on to discover the secrets to attaining true love. It's your natural state of being, and one we all must evolve towards.

Let go of the need to be normal and step into what naturally awaits you by surrendering to the truths of love.

If You Don't Know, It's a No

There is no issue with meeting and dating different people to make it possible for love to enter your life. However, we often persist in romantic relationships for too long, as we try and work out if we are in love with someone.

All choices are valid, but when it comes to love, if you don't know after a reasonable period whether it's present, it's most likely not.

Attraction is different. It can ebb and flow with circumstances as they change. Both partners can effectively alter it.

But when it comes to love, if you don't know whether you love someone, it's normally a no.

Love is the True Healer

How often have you heard the expression that time heals all wounds? This is another fallacy. Love is what heals all wounds. It is the ultimate healer. Time is no more than the passing of thought and our way of measuring and organising our lives.

When our bodies sustain injuries or diseases, we are so often healed naturally. For example, cuts and bruises are eventually resolved by our bodies. But what do you think does that healing – the body or some magical force within it?

Truly, it's the magical force of infinite intelligence. Our souls provide the subconscious energies and infinite intelligences required to heal your body. It's not AI (Artificial Intelligence), its II (our Intuitive Intelligence) that does the healing. We just trust the wisdom in our bodies to heal us.

Even when a surgeon operates on your physical body, he is merely the worthy assistant of the inner intelligence or awareness provided by our souls. He puts your body in a better physical position so that the power of love can take over and finish the job. It is a force of nature with endless powers that we only vaguely understand.

Time heals nothing.

Even psychological wounds can be healed through the magic mirror of love, when we let ourselves witness the wisdom in any reflection it brings to our attention.

Ask for love's help to heal you and heal it will, for your soul is your centre of love and it is waiting for you to invite it fully into your experiences.

But beware, this healing process could come with a need to face current or suppressed pain, for that is so often the doorway to freedom.

In the song 'The Way We Were' made famous by Barbra Streisand, there is a recognition that when a memory is too painful to remember, we often choose to simply forget it. But beware: pain may be out of mind, but it so often does not go away until we face it and learn its lessons.

I spent many years learning to feel and then face my pain, which I was receiving as messages of love from my soul. Ironically, when I learned to love my pain, it gave me the wisdom to heal.

My book *From Pain to Possibility* gives much more detail on this.

The Unlimited Power of Love

There are many stories and songs about the power of love, but they can never quite express in fullness the extent of love's power.

Love in its absolute power can create another human being.

Love's true power is absolute because it is of infinite intelligence.

When we measure the intelligence of a human, we often talk of IQ, or their intelligence quotient. Highly intelligent people are said to have an IQ in the range of 145 to 160. Now compare that to infinity. There's no competition really!

The universe is comprised of love as is the natural planet that we are inhabiting. Mother Nature is a conscious being, like you and I. Love is the source of everything and, at its core, the universe was created from nothing but the love and intelligence of God.

When we allow love to be the core energy of our relationships, and not our ego-based thoughts, our relationships have unlimited potential.

This applies to everything in our lives – our careers, hobbies, friendships, and so on. When we live in the energy of love, anything and everything is possible.

Isn't it time we started to live from love in all that we do?

It's how I endeavour to live my life now, every single day.

To do this we must learn to stop thinking as much as we do and start feeling our way forward. After all, love will remind your mind of what truly matters, if you let it.

Our feelings are the only place where love can be found, and where its whispers can be heard.

CHAPTER 2

An Analogy for Love

The River of Love

To conceptualise how important love is to our very existence, let us compare life to a raindrop.

We begin our lives as a raindrop falling from the clouds above. We are individual drops, yet not alone in undertaking our return to the planet we call Earth, for we are surrounded by other raindrops also falling. We have probably done this repeatedly before now, having lived past lives, it's just that now we have chosen to re-enter Earth at this particular moment. It's no coincidence. It is divine.

So now we are fresh as a new source of life and love. As an infant raindrop, we are innocent and vulnerable as we join the river below. We know not what lies ahead. But we are full of curiosity and alive with the possibilities that await, for we are open to explore and ready to flow with our feelings.

We still hold the loving energies and joyous intent we remember from the home we have left behind, though not conscious of the truth behind our arrival and the duality instilled within us. We have little to no memory of our previous visits to the planet (or whether this is our first time), and this amnesia is both a gift and a debt we will have to circumnavigate as our lives unfold. For now, we are simply ready to flow and experience the wonder of life on a new adventure. We are vibrating as pure love, and ready to be truly loved in return. Our purity is clear for all to see and feel.

We are whole like a raindrop, ready to become a part of the river of life, and flow with the energy of those we must trust in the initial stages of our journey.

But this is where it can all go horribly wrong. As the river flows through the terrain it encounters, its journey is subject to the natural landscapes around it. Sometimes there may be rapids, sometimes the river will meander through peaceful landscapes, and sometimes it may become stagnant in the absence of the energies it needs to move through. Yet it will ultimately keep moving towards the sea, where it will return to a much bigger source of energy.

Along the way the river will also encounter new energies that project it forward towards its next experience. Rain and fresh waters will join from creeks and tributaries, giving us the impetus to grow and enhance our rate of flow. New relationships are key examples of these new energies that will greet us along our journey.

Sometimes the water in the river will separate and flow in different directions around islands and new land masses. That water may even carve a new path, then return and reunite back into the original river. Or it may continue a separate path at the behest of nature.

The water in the original river will reach the sea in its own good time, untroubled by its passage and progress. It knows not what lies around the next bend, until it unfolds.

Once in the sea, the water then moves with the prevailing currents and winds, sustaining life, until it eventually succumbs to the power of the sun and returns to where it came from, as evaporation takes over.

As is the river, as are our lives.

We are the droplets of unconditional love, and we flow as nature intends.

Our relationships in life are like the different terrains that the river encounters along the way. They burst forth and cease through the power of truth, and because of the power of love we know not where they are taking us until we get there. We can thus never anticipate when and where love will arise, and whether a relationship will enhance our flow, stagnate us, or challenge us to grow. Sometimes relationships can even bring forth new life or create new flows of self-expression.

Although many of us may want a smooth passage straight to the sea, is that really the point of life?

Love may have other ideas for us, and impose its will upon our many twists and turns. We are truly at its behest.

The ultimate outcome is the same, but the winding nature of the journey is different for every raindrop, for all are unique, yet all are united in the body of water that we define as the river.

How your life flows will be determined by the energy of love, and how you move through the experiences that you encounter. Will you move as love decrees, or in resistance to its very presence, lessons and delights?

The choice is yours!

CHAPTER 3

Your Absolute Connection to Love

As Above, So Below

Spiritual followers often speak of living in the energy of 'As Above, So Below.' This expression refers to a person who knows the full truth of themselves. They know that they are living in both a 3D or physical reality and a metaphysical reality, at the same time, until they die.

When they die, they then simply exit the 3D reality and remain only in the metaphysical reality.

Whether you believe this or not, it doesn't matter, because the truth is still the truth. We *are* all living in the 'As Above, So Below' paradigm, whether we accept it or not.

Love is the same, in that it arises in metaphysical realms and manifests into the physical realms. It arises on a universal level, as it is the pure energy of God, or the universe. At the same time, it is also expressed into and through the physical world we live in. When we live a life on Earth, we are a vessel of pure love created by consciousness itself – we have been manifested into the form that our souls want us to be in this incarnation.

Thus, we are all at the centre point of the 'As Above, So Below' reality. Once we realise this fully and connect to the love that is the creator within us, we can live a life with full awareness of the love that we are, and this allows us to create the life we desire by channelling our love into the world.

We have two operating systems, as I mentioned above, through which we can make choices or decisions: our minds (or egos) and our souls (or hearts). Unfortunately, our minds have limited intelligence and only know what they are taught in each incarnation, so unless they become connected to the soul, they can only operate as rudimentary memory banks that remember past experiences and the lessons we have been shown by life. They can derive new ideas from past understandings, but new paradigms of thought usually arise from new levels of consciousness.

Our souls, however, are connected to the infinite intelligence of the universe, through the universal field of intelligence. Our heart chakras (not our physical hearts for they are just muscles) provide this connection back to God. Our souls only know love in its purest form, and only express as love, with love and for love.

So which operating system do you think we should trust the most, especially when it comes to manifesting what we want from life? And which system may work better in a romantic relationship, where love and passion are so sought after?

Unfortunately, in this life, very few minds witness or recognise the 'As Above, So Below' paradigm, and are instead totally focussed on the 'So Below' portion, being the physical world that we inhabit. This is just a conditioned way of being as this is the version of our lives that most people are taught to believe in and experience every day.

Resistance to our soul energy being the eternal truth of us is normal, although this understanding is starting to breakdown across the world, as people awaken to the truth of themselves and the power of unity consciousness – being the understanding that we are all connected by love in the universal field.

It is possible to breakdown this resistance completely and live predominantly from soul energy, and 'earth it' into our physical lives, connecting with our own pure love. This is an advanced state to be in. But this can involve much personal inner work.

My book, *From Pain to Possibility*, teaches the natural path to this holy place, which is open to everyone.

We tend to think of the process of becoming holy as something set aside for prophets and angels, but it is possible for all humans to enter this extraordinary place whilst still alive on Earth in our current bodies. We can master both the physical and metaphysical realms simultaneously if we choose to be guided by the love already within us.

Few make this choice, because the path to becoming multidimensional in this way is not widely understood, even by many spiritual people. Some call it 'coming home' or 'enlightenment', others call it a form of reincarnation because essentially you are arising from the ashes of your previous illusions of self, like the mythical Phoenix, and must allow your old identity, or ego, to essentially 'die' and rest in peace, whilst you live on in your current body.

Letting an identity go that you have spent a lifetime creating, and may have served you well, is one of the hardest and most disorientating things for a human being to do, which is why it is rare. It can be a while until your true personality emerges from your soul energy, as you follow this rebirth path.

And yet, love can show us the way, for living from our true state as pure love is the absolute, or most advanced, state any human being can attain. Indeed, in a world that is constantly trying to teach you who you are, only love can show you what you are. And from this place of absolute clarity, you will find the true you – and your true who.

The Infinite Possibilities of Love

Figure 2 below illustrates where you currently exist in the absolute centre of the metaphysical or higher dimensional realms, and the 3D physical reality here on Earth, where we have been manifested into life by our metaphysical souls:

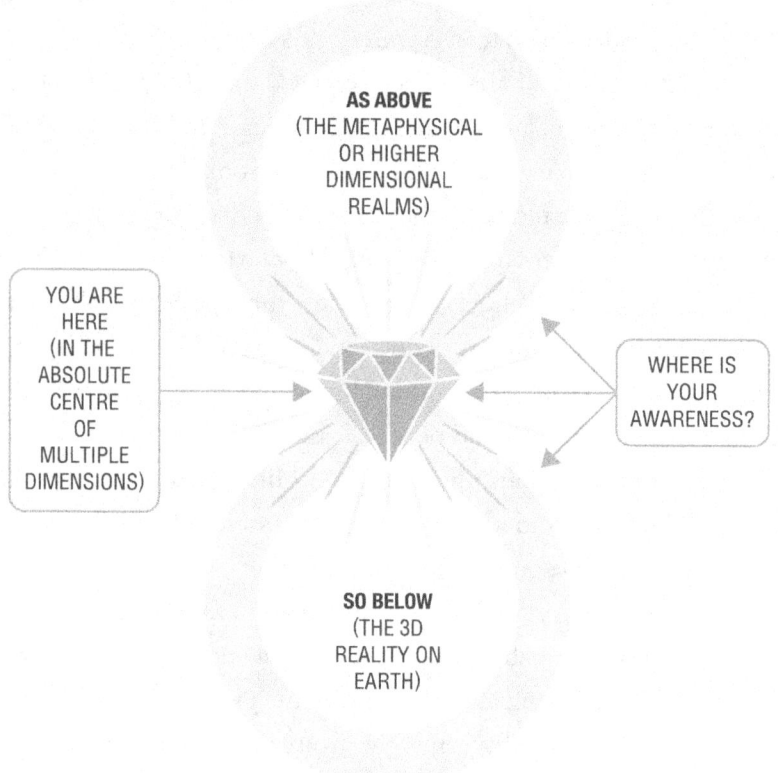

Figure 2: As Above, So Below

The universal symbol of infinity, standing vertically, represents the depths of our human experience, and how we communicate with the universe whilst alive in physical form on this planet. We are always in full connection with the universe, or divine energies, for we inhabit the intersecting point where both parts of the symbol connect. We are like a crystal-clear diamond in the centre of these dimensions, able to receive and reflect light and love.

As light and love penetrate through our human selves, we can then choose to earth these beautiful energies into our 3D world. Indeed, we are constantly receiving vibrations of love from the universe through our souls and our chakra systems, and can manifest them all into our 3D reality should we choose to do so.

Yet most people remain within their conscious limitations, for they only see themselves as inhabiting the bottom of the symbol, their 3D world.

Then again, some spiritually minded people can become obsessed with the top of the symbol, retreating from the 3D world that they exist within, to find solace in deflecting themselves from their dual reality.

I spent the first 53 years of my life largely unaware of the metaphysical realities of myself. After a major awakening process this all changed, and I spent the next 10+years learning all I could about the metaphysical. And I loved it!

However, I am acutely aware that I can't just live in one realm or the other. I am a part of both as, essentially, I am a spirit living a human life.

We are not here on this planet to think that we operate solely in the top or the bottom of this symbol. We are here to become aware that we are connected to both and can manifest our 3D lives through the power of love and infinite intelligence. From here we can create the lives that our souls want us to connect to and manifest, which we can do once our bodies and minds take the respective actions they need to take to manifest this love into our 3D reality, such that we act as a vessel for love to flow through, like big diamonds.

Did you know that the word 'astronaut' means a sailor of the celestial realms? In a way, we are all akin to metaphysical sailors, who have decided to land on this Earth and explore its varied terrain. We wear a physical suit like an astronaut, but deep within that suit of protection is our pure essence of love.

The love that we are has chosen this adventure with passion and for learning, and we can either resist this experiment, or relax knowing that all we ever wanted is already within us, and that we are always being watched over by the mother ship, even though it is hard to see at times.

For thousands of years, humanity has feared the 'As Above'. We have considered it to be the domain of the dead or spirits. Many think it's where we go when we die, entering either heaven or hell.

We both fear it and revere it, not realising that we never left it, and that we remain connected to it forever. We can never sever this connection, because all souls are omnipresent, meaning that they can traverse the universe as they desire. Yours has chosen to manifest some of its energies as you on Earth, right now.

When we surrender to the flow of love that is within us and allow it to manifest our heart's true desires, we can create our own version of heaven on Earth. These desires are, put simply, the will of God.

All we need to do, as individuals or collectively, is to choose to live from our hearts in union within ourselves, and with others, not from our minds in the illusion of separation.

If you look around this world at present, do you think enough people are living from their hearts, in the energy of love? You be the judge!

Our Earth-Bound Challenges

Being able to live in the pure energy of love on Earth has some intended energetic challenges or barriers, which many of us need to overcome should we choose to return to love.

Let me be clear, you cannot do this by just thinking it is so. There is a path most of us must take – from understanding ourselves as love, to knowing ourselves as such, and then allowing ourselves to embody this reality. The process back to embodying love is one of learning of and eliminating any illusions that tell us we are not.

My book *From Pain to Possibility* outlines this is detail.

Specifically, there are some core energies that cause life on Earth to feel like a harsh and testing experience at times and exaggerate our feelings of separation from love. Most of them we have inherited, and are not easy to overcome, despite being largely illusory.

The key factors are:

1. Our own limiting egoic thoughts and beliefs. These can harbour fears, validations and needs that stifle our ability to love and value ourselves. Most of these have been learned from a world that lacks sufficient self-awareness to know thyself. My book *Where Your Happiness Hides* explores this area more deeply.

2. Our lack of comprehension that we are frequencies first and human beings second. Essentially, we are light beings who are being human temporarily. Our ignorance of this reality has led us to ignore how important it is to prioritise the frequency of love that we are.

We can influence our frequencies, however, when we know how to do so, and take the bold but natural steps to prioritise this important process. Many spiritual people are in the process of working on this reality, so that they can return to their multidimensional selves, but it is not mainstream practice.

Our frequency influences the quality of our lives, including the relationships we can foster and maintain. All is frequency at the end of the day.

3. Karmic energies that are Earth-bound only and have been created in this life, or by previous incarnations of our souls. At some stage we may be called upon to rebalance these often-dense energies by our souls.

Often there is a strong correlation between these first two energies.
 Let's explore them all a little further…

1. Our own limiting egoic thoughts and beliefs

Although, inherently, we all know that love is what we seek, our minds have been conditioned to think that we will be more lovable if we attain more success and avoid failure, and this conditioning has led us away from love in search of poor surrogates, such as money, sex and power.

Our egos will always protect and project us. Accordingly, at one end of the spectrum they want us to be safe and secure. And at the other end of the spectrum, they drive us to be successful, beautiful, rich, important and admired.

Is it any wonder that our egos also drive us to find romantic partners with these same qualities? After all, if our partner is rich, successful and beautiful don't our egos help us to feel even safer and more valued?

And yet your partner is not you!

The love in our hearts has a different agenda. It wants us to be happy, healthy, fearless, joyful, compassionate and fun. Love is naturally creative but does not create with the intention of achieving more or making you more important. It cares less about that agenda. It wants you to *be* more, not *own* more. Love is already everything and wants nothing more than to just be allowed to fill you with infinite possibilities and joyous expression.

This conundrum creates a deep confusion within us that we have lost the wisdom to witness. It is highly subconscious in most people.

Intense pain from my perceived failures has driven me to explore and witness these realities for myself. But I'm now so glad that it did, because living from love is what is important, not achieving importance itself.

If we can remember the true love that we already are, we can't help but to create the life we always secretly wanted but never dared to dream into reality. Remembering the real agenda back to love can thus set us free and take us from confusion to clarity – a clarity that will bring forth our greatest happiness.

Your path back to love is your eternal destiny. It's your heart's only true desire. It cares less about success and does not fear any form of failure. In fact, it does not know the meaning of this word, for once you are in the feeling of love all the time you will feel complete. And you don't need any other person or achievement to do this for you.

In this vaulted place, you can focus totally on finding happiness and fulfilment in your life. The pressure to win and not lose is gone. This is where peace lies.

Your soul knows when you will return to this wonderful energy, so trust it. It may be in this life, or it may be in the next, it doesn't matter – because all is a journey, and that journey is why we are here. Love itself will take you on this journey home to your true self if you let it take the reins – all you need to do is ask. It is waiting for your request.

Allow, intend and you shall receive, it's that simple.

And once you arrive home, you won't care how long or how hard your journey home was, because the truth of your own love, and the feelings that follow, will feel like nothing you have ever known before.

Becoming no-thing (i.e. love) will take you home to everything!

And when you realise that, in the energy of pure love, you are a part of everything, you will need nothing else.

You deserve to have this awareness. It is your truth.

2. We Are Frequencies

As outlined earlier, many people don't realise that we are frequencies first and foremost, so they certainly don't understand that their individual frequency at any given point can attract or repel others with the same or different frequencies.

But once we accept this, we can also accept that we can adjust our frequencies, and thus our inner realities can impact our outer realities.

Our beliefs, both conscious and subconscious, can thus have a direct correlation to the energy we bring to this world and the energies that we attract towards us. They influence how we interact with others and how we feel about ourselves, because our frequency, or resonance, is directly influenced by the beliefs that we hold, and the associated energies that flow from these beliefs.

Many of us have become conditioned from childhood, and this continues as we age, to believe whatever we are taught to believe, and have not been encouraged to own the process of determining our own beliefs for ourselves. Our inherent curiosity has been replaced by compliance. We are strongly influenced by the views and beliefs of our parents, and the society of which we are a part.

As an infant we are usually in the energy of innocence. We are naturally programmed for fun, learning and adventure. However, we soon learn that our way to survival and recognition is to follow the wishes and demands of our carers. After all, as a baby and young infant we learn that our very survival is dependent on our parents and/or carers. We don't want to die – as this is the biggest primal fear of a human being – so we fit in and seek security and love through compliance with the rules of our providers.

But by deciding to adopt 'the way things are done around here', we are prone to move away from our truths, self-trust and self-acceptance. The true self within us that knows what we love to do, but what we want to become is suppressed, and the human ego inflates itself by thinking that it is the source of consciousness, rather than understanding that our heart is truly our centre of conscious awareness, and therefore love.

Some people are fortunate to be brought up by carers or parents who encourage individual self-expression and authentic expansion. But they are the fortunate few.

Dysfunctional families will of course have different impacts on different children, but the damage is always profound when it stops a child from becoming their true self. This process of disassociation from self not only damages a person's self-esteem and can lead them into a life of inauthentic expression and limited levels of self-love, it is the genesis of our belief in separation.

We become what we are taught to be, not what we are here to be.

The damage is done. Our inner reality is one of separation, and so our outer reality must align. The unity within our mind, body and spirit as one whole being is lost in the illusion that our hearts do not matter.

Ironically, we then also come to believe that we need to prove that we are lovable, rather than just being the love that we already are. As our souls and their loving messages are ignored in our lives, we lose awareness of what really matters to us and what will make us happy.

By ceasing to feel the love in our hearts, though, we can't help but dim the light and love that we are, which limits the quality of our relationships, for what we put out in life we get back.

When you pare away all the noise we encounter in our lives, we are pure love and light, and this is what makes us lovable, not some big house or flash title. Perhaps it's time we understood this truth and embodied it.

3. Earth-Bound Karmic Energies

Life on Earth is unique for, whilst we are here, we are burdened by karmic energies that must eventually be cleared. These, like conditioned beliefs, impact on our sense of freedom to love ourselves and others.

This topic is explored more deeply in Chapter 11, for it is somewhat advanced and esoteric.

The Relationship Between Our Karmic Energies and Our Greatest Sin

Humanity has adopted a plethora of definitions of what constitutes sin. We have created rules and laws that we think will give us order and harmony.

However, our greatest sin has been forgetting what we truly are, and going off in search of who we think we should be. This has led us astray and into a fearful and often chaotic world.

We have created many laws and rules, but how effectively are they working to create order and harmony?

But if we can collectively remember the truth of our being and return to pure love, one soul at a time, imagine how many other so-called sins might cease to pollute our world and our happiness?

Love is ultimately the answer to everything we seek. And once we find it within ourselves there will be no question that we are home. We will cease to experience fear as we have known it before, for we will understand that this was always God's plan. He has such wondrous plans for us; we don't need our own!

So let us start by remembering that we are multidimensional beings who have chosen to live an Earth-bound life, to learn and to evolve ourselves. The state of living as a multidimensional being is not a myth. It is what we already are. We just don't realise it on a mass scale.

If you make the choice to find your full awareness as the diamond in the centre of our different dimensions, you can and will do this. After all, it is your ultimate destiny.

There are many books and experts out there, like me, who can help you rebalance your karmic energies and make your journey home. But of course you need to desire it. Either way, your choice is valid.

Arriving at this place of full awareness does, however, take some inner work for most of us, depending on how many conditioned beliefs and negative karmic energies you hold within your being.

It is possible to live more from the energy of your heart, without going all the way to the awareness of your multidimensionality, or universal awareness. This is what many spiritual people also do.

Any shift closer to your soul-energy, and away from your ego, can only assist you to find greater peace in your life.

To make this journey I had many illusions to face and clear, to align my energies fully with the love flowing through me. Most people on an advanced awareness journey are in this place. I did enjoy it, for what could be more important and valuable to understand than your truth.

Essentially, this journey is about learning through the power of love what you are not, so you can then be shown what you are. This is the path back to your truth.

Your soul may have done this before on the Earth plane, and it may have been waiting for you to come with it on this journey of remembering, for truly that's all it is.

Until you tame your ego, it most likely will be the biggest barrier to your soul energy becoming your dominant source of being.

Why Would I Want to Do All This?

Living from love is your natural state. Most people on Earth constantly experience a battle between their hearts and minds. This battle, like most battles, can be very painful.

Mine was, because my soul kept bringing me back to my divine life plan with a thud, every time I moved away from what my soul came here to experience. This led to much loss in my life as I was essentially redirected in painful ways.

Some readers may have had a similar experience in their lives. If your soul is here to experience a significant level of conscious expansion in this life and your ego takes you in another direction, you will almost certainly experience significant moments of pain and change. But the combined momentum of these moments is your ticket to significant personal transformation.

You were manifested onto this planet to reconnect to your truths. This is where sickness, ageing, ignorance and unhappiness become things of the past, for the more you align with the energy of your soul, the more you become its inherent energies.

And the more closely you connect to the pure frequency of love within you, the more loving will be your relationships with others, particularly your romantic partners.

We all want really satisfying relationships in our lives. With love inspiring our lives and our relationships we can't help but have relationships that continually grow and expand.

As the universe constantly expands and creates through the infinite power of love, so can we. And the biggest obstacle to this inspiring place is your own mind, and its lack of awareness of what love is and what it can bring into your life, when you simply surrender to its wonderful powers.

The journey back to this place is fascinating and may require you to face the pain that the previous resistance of your ego has put in the way of your homecoming. Everyone's journey home is different and can never be compared to another's.

But we can all open the gate to a better place of living. This gate is made of love, and only love can take you through it when you are ready to surrender to its magic.

Mastering the 3D world and the metaphysical realms together is a challenge that is open to us all should we want to do so. And you can do it with a loving partner and others if you choose to. Or you can do it alone.

This journey is not for everyone, yet. But it will be, for that is the future of life on this planet, as love increasingly asserts itself and takes humanity into new paradigms.

Why would it do this? Because it is 'time' and many souls are ready and yearning for this magical experience!

CHAPTER 4

The Critical Importance of Self-Love

The Most Important Relationship of All

We all want to be loved by others. We are infatuated with this romantic experience, for it can feel wonderful. It's intoxicating, particularly in the early stages.

However, there is a far more important love that we truly need to value, but so often don't, and that is the love that we have within and for ourselves.

Spiritual books are full of this concept of self-love. However, it is not part of our normal vernacular, for we often think of a person with high self-esteem as someone who is arrogant. They may just be self-centred in a healthy way, and love themselves.

The reality is that finding self-love is vastly more difficult than finding another person to love you, even though it is the only love that you can truly rely upon for the rest of your life, and develop at your own discretion, and in your own timing.

My journey back to self-love and higher self-worth was incredibly difficult and required me to overcome a web of limiting beliefs and negative feelings about myself. But I'll never regret it, for it opened me a much higher sense of self-confidence and self-worth.

Self-love is within your own hands, if you seek to take this valuable step forward in life, for it is the essence of you.

Once attained, self-love is incredibly precious, for your ability to manifest a life you love comes from this amazing state of being. It can't come from outside of you, for that is generally impossible.

It is not someone else's job to love you either, as they could choose at any time to take their love away from you and direct it elsewhere. And, as we all know, this can be extremely painful and confusing.

What they were offering you may not have even been love. Or it may have been an impure love, damaged by their ego or personal attachment styles.

There is another truth at play here, though, that is not well understood – the reality is that no other person can ever love you more than you can love yourself. Why? Because you can only ever feel your own love in a loving relationship. You can't *own* the feelings of another person. What you *can* feel is only your feelings.

Your mind will resist this statement because we are conditioned to believe otherwise. We often rely on receiving what we think is the love of another to make us feel whole in our hearts and fully cherished.

However, a universal principle of life on this planet that we need to collectively embrace and appreciate is that the love in our hearts is a frequency, as outlined above. Thus, all that another person's love and attention is doing is helping you to feel your own frequency of love and fill the illusory hole in your heart that you think exists. It truly doesn't! Your heart always was and always will be whole. It's only your conditioned thoughts and negative energies that tell you that you are not fully lovable. These are just illusions of the mind. Your soul loves you more than your mind could ever comprehend!

A person's projection of love towards you may allow you to feel a lesser shadow across your heart, but that person cannot fill your heart with the frequency it desires to feel whole, as that must come from you.

Essentially, therefore, you determine the level of love that you can feel, whether you're alone or in a relationship. No one else can own it for you.

Again, let that sink in! You won't get that from a movie!

This is one reason why the euphoria of a new love can feel so short lived – because the boost is mental, not enshrined in your own self-love. It gives your mental self-image a lift and allows you to forget (for a period) that you have limiting thoughts and beliefs that diminish your self-love. But the other person is simply deflecting you temporarily from your inner pain.

When a new love commences in our lives, most of us go through the same mental process that goes like this: "I have met the love of my life. They must be my soul mate. This is it. I am in love and this love will last forever. I am the luckiest person in the world".

Ring any bells?

Accordingly, we almost immediately go into planning mode. We plan a new future, based on our conditioned romantic expectations. We quickly plan a mental image of our wedding, where we could live and how many kids we will have together. Does that sound familiar too?

We focus on the other person's physicality and our shared interests. We are well and truly wearing rose-coloured glasses as we do this, pushing aside the negatives as irrelevant or easy to overcome. And maybe they are. But maybe the main negatives, or red flags as we call them, are just not on show yet, or we have chosen to ignore them because we have waited too long to be in love.

We often try to be what our new lover wants us to be and move away from our authentic selves in the hope that we have found the person of our dreams.

Why do we do this?

As a rule, we are conditioned to seek the safety and security of a romantic relationship and the more we are polarised to that person, the safer we feel in that arrangement.

But we have not stopped, gone inward or accessed our hearts to see if a real soul connection is present. The dopamine has most likely kicked in and we are hoping and thinking that 'true love' is present. Finally, we are the central character in our own fairy tale. Euphoria and sexual connections become the dominant bonds, and we become the epitome of the 'hopeless romantic' – we forget that sexuality is one of our favourite ways of expressing love, but it is NOT love and never can be.

In my life, I have had several relationships, but often I did not see that love was not deeply present until I went inward, usually months later, and felt deeply into my heart.

This was hard on me and others, because I was engaged in a relationship that was truly not of the purity of love that my heart was seeking. Of course I was on the receiving end as well of these delayed decisions, so I speak with experience on this matter.

I also had a few relationships where I mistook intimacy and sexual passion for love. These were valuable lessons that I now treasure for they taught me much.

So let us be clear, you can never be loved at a higher vibration than you love yourself. This makes it important to find the purest level of self-love that you can within yourself, so that your external relationships can be purer as well, and therefore more satisfying.

This makes it extremely important, when a relationship ends, to consider how your personal beliefs and behaviours limited the success of that relationship, and how you might yet evolve through the experience, so that next time the same problems don't arise. Jumping straight back into a relationship without doing this soul-searching only means you're still vulnerable to the same dangers.

After my second divorce, I went to see a dating agency. The lady running the agency advised me not to date again until I had moved through my grief and found my heart again. This was a profound piece of advice that I will always be grateful for.

Find the flame of love in your heart and the flame of another can equally grace you with its presence. And this understanding is the gateway to understanding true love, and why it is so rare in this wounded world.

Of course, many people will meet the love of their life and create a wonderful union that lasts for many years. These types of soul contracts are truly 'written in the stars' before we are born.

When we are born, we do have a divine plan for our lives, which our hearts have essentially agreed to. Our hearts will then invite in what we need to realise this plan; we need only to listen and learn.

The only exception would be if you are not meant to clear issues and wounds in this incarnation around romantic energies. In that case, you will most likely not be tested in this area by your soul and circumstances. You may have already worked through these types of experiences in a 'past life' and mastered them, or perhaps they are yet to come.

Either way, we get what we need to experience to advance our soul's consciousness in each life, and often that will involve matters of romance, as well as other areas of your life, like money or your career. Most tests will then point us back to the attainment of a higher sense of self-love and self-worth.

Why Self-Love Sets the Tone

The universe is aptly named, for it represents one big song or verse. The letters 'uni' when used in a combining phrase mean 'one' or 'having only one'. 'Verse' is then a word often used with respect to music or poetry. Hence, the 'universe' is comprised of many tunes for all beings within it, with each having their own unique frequency or pitch, then combining to form a song, the vibration of which is beyond our comprehension, though some call it 'ohm'.

You are part of this giant tune, not only when you are in the metaphysical, but also when you are alive on this third-dimensional planet Earth.

Earth is a special place in the cosmos, because when you are here in form, your frequency can be altered by past experiences or karma.

Your true vibration of self is toned down by conditioned beliefs and energies that make our lives denser than that of your soul in the ether. But as stated above, you can remember your true self.

The wisdom of this has been largely lost for centuries in what has been called the 'Kali Yuga', which refers to a period on Earth where ignorant and limited thinking created a dark age, or period of disconnection from our truths. This lowered the collective vibration of humanity and took us further away from love as a collective.

We are now exiting this era and entering an era of much higher vibration. This lift in vibration is intended by God, for the impurity of love on Earth is impacting negatively on our planet and other civilisations that we inhabit in the galaxy.

How can this be possible, you may ask?

It is the reality of what is called 'oneness' and the energetic connectivity of all, and it means that an opportunity now exists for everyone on Earth to take the journey back to pure love and become their true frequency of self. You already are it; you just can't get to it until you clear away the energetic barriers to it.

This journey will be different for every soul on the planet, depending on the density of their karmic field and the vibration that they are trying to return to.

So, how do these vibrational realities influence your ability to take your life to a higher level?

Your inner vibration or self-esteem influences everything and is crucial to your journey. It determines what gets attracted into your periphery, and in turn influences the quality of your life. Your level of self-love is essentially a measure of the purity of the vibration in your soul that you can perceive.

The reality is that your self-love was never taken from you, it just got covered up by any negative energies that you harboured within you. And some of these are hard to get at for they were established in past incarnations. However, the experiences in your current incarnation will normally be a great guide to what you are being urged to clear in this life by your soul. Clearing these energies – through self-reflection, awareness and self-forgiveness – will not only remove energetic barriers you may be going through to experience the purity of self-love but can also clear karmic energies.

As soon as I was able to, I took this one step further and worked with high vibrational beings and people who were able to clear my major past life karmas and cleanse my energy field. This was a choice that I was driven to make by my own heart.

The higher the vibration that you bring to your life, the more love that you can enjoy and attract into your life. Your resistance to good things – that you are truly worthy of, and that the universe wants you to have – is dissolved in this process, since you simply cannot be loved by another beyond the level of self-love that you possess within your being.

This is why deep inner work is required if you want to improve the quality of your love life, or your life in general, without introducing the fragility of a life lived from ego.

We are all manifesting in our 3D lives all the time, but when we are manifesting from our ego-centric minds – whether by employing conditioned responses to present challenges or reviewing challenges that we experienced earlier in our current lives – we open ourselves up to being 'shunted back' to a different way of being if our energies do not align with love.

The more negatively conditioned you are and continue to allow yourself to be, the more negative any experiences you encounter in your future will be. Firstly because you are attracting it, and secondly because the soul wants you to learn from the negative experiences that have arisen and will continue to arise.

Those experiences will also continue to plague any current relationships, because we have been conditioned to view them as having been done to us, rather than for and through us, and this negative view of experiences blinds us to the love that we all are, taints the purity of the love that we could experience, and limits the love we can therefore attract into our lives.

Thus, while you might be attractive to some people, your ability to be loved is essentially impaired by your lack of self-love, and you will only attract the purity of love that matches yours.

With the benefit of my current wisdom, I now know that the fragile romantic relationships I experienced in my life, which ended in pain, occurred for purpose – so that I could expand my consciousness and level of self-love. I now understand that this was my destiny and not a series of failures, as I once thought. They were lessons I needed to go through. And it has set me up for higher vibrational experiences of love in my future. I am now grateful that these powerful steps graced my path for me to traverse, and I forgive myself for ever feeling otherwise.

Indeed, as mentioned above, a great way to start increasing our self-love is to self-reflect and forgive ourselves. Forgiveness is a critical element of the journey to higher self-love and to the gift of being able to find peace in seemingly difficult circumstances (such as where our egos are or have been challenged).

To forgive yourself or another, it is best to drop into the energy of your soul, since love is always able to forgive, whereas our egos struggle to do this effectively.

Quiet meditation may help, as can consciously relating with others.

Asking for forgiveness from your heart may also provide you with the peace that you seek. The ego cannot do this easily, especially when the peace you seek relates to ended relationships, for the ego is usually the centre of the pain in any relationship separation and wants to project and protect your side of the story.

But the quicker we can develop our self-love, the quicker we can rebalance our frequencies and attract into our lives the frequencies our heart truly deserves to encounter and enjoy.

The Illusion of Self-Worth

People often speak of self-worth in the same context of self-love, for they are closely linked. Your sense of self-worth is influenced by the level of self-love you feel, and can extend to yourself. It is the inherent value you can place on your own self.

However, the concept of measuring a person's self-worth is an illusion of the egoic mind. It is truly a pointless exercise.

If we are all pure love at the core and all children of the universe – manifested by our souls, so that they can go through different experiences on Earth – our worth is immeasurable, and truly cannot be diminished by anyone's thoughts, including your own.

To use a commonly heard expression 'we are all equal in the eyes of God'. We are all a part of a universe that loves us, and which we can never leave. Essentially, we are a single tune within the one big tune of the universe, but a unique one.

The universe would be incomplete without any of us, no matter who we are or what we do.

Yet, if this is the truth of life, why do we so often depreciate ourselves and our true value to the world?

The answer lies in our ignorance of these truths, and in the fact that we are prone to rate or judge each other on a continuous basis. And we do this rating because it's a learned way of living. We grow up in a world full of constant judgements and rankings. It's hard to escape, so we normally just adopt the same practice. We don't consider the internal light that we all possess, we judge a person on non-sensible aspects of their life that belie the understanding that we are merely living an experience that our souls have chosen for us.

In one life you may be a king or a queen, and in the next life you may be a pauper. This is the soul's choice, not your mind's choice. You were born into the family that your soul chose. Of course, you can change your life circumstances, but if that is possible then it will just be another choice to rise above our previous situation.

We so often rate people on material things that are outside of them, such as their wealth, job, title, partner, or the size of the house they live in. These are interesting things to talk about, but they don't matter as much as the thing that isn't matter – the love that they are.

Unfortunately, the greatest critic of ourselves is usually us. We put the same lens across ourselves as we do to others, except normally the ratings scale is much harsher, because so many of us are brought up to believe that we should not fail, and that we must be perfect to be lovable.

But this is us looking into cracked mirrors that distort our true magnificence! We are miracles of creation, for we are pure love, whether we can witness it or not – we just are!

Of course, no one can be perfect, and a person's personal circumstances are NOT them. They are external to them.

I spent many years suffering from a sense of low self-worth, until I began to understand the truth of life on Earth, and the realities of love.

After two divorces, lost jobs and associated reductions in my personal wealth, I learned to look at myself through the lens of love. Love never judges so why should I?

Again, a person's external achievements may change the extent to which other people are attracted to them, but it can never change their true and intrinsic value, for regardless of circumstances that remains absolute, like the diamond in the centre of the infinity symbol shown above. Their hearts are flawless.

So, the next time you find yourself self-deprecating, stop and consider the lack of wisdom in this process. You are love, which makes you everything and nothing all at once. And everyone is the same.

So, lets drop the nebulous rankings and ignorant judgements.

Is it Best to Be Single or Attached?

Sometimes self-love can be found more readily when we separate ourselves temporarily from the egos of others and allow ourselves to do the deep inner work that is so often needed to feel our own love, and to discover its true power.

In a busy world where judgements abound, removing unnecessary judgements by avoiding them temporarily can allow the process of returning to your true sense of self-love to unfold with greater clarity and less external 'noise'.

If you have supportive friends, family members or a partner who is open to helping you with your personal growth, being single or alone may not be a suitable personal status to adopt. It is all a matter of personal circumstances.

Most people prefer to be in secure loving relationships if they can be, rather than single, as this is a norm.

But I have found that extended periods of being single, and even isolated, have helped me to delve deeply into my own limiting beliefs that had tended to diminish my self-esteem. In such a place, I learned to care for myself and enjoy my own company.

There was a part of me that always wanted a loving partner, of course, but I also knew my deep inner work would be a potential burden on a partner who was not open to this important form of self-enquiry.

After all, much of what was required of me entailed facing and processing the pain of past issues, fears, attachments and traumas. I did not want to impose that on another who was not ready to support it.

This was a conscious choice that I made to fast track my journey to appreciating and connecting to the true depth of my self-love.

There are times in your life when being single or alone is in your best interests, but there are also times when a loving partner or friend can help you grow much more effectively. It's just a personal choice, in a life defined by a series of choices.

Ultimately, expanding your sense of self-love and self-worth are critical to inviting greater love into your life.

Note the use of the words 'sense of' here, because that's all it is. Your true worth and the love within your heart are never diminished. We just think they are.

Just remember, no one deserves to be loved more than you!

CHAPTER 5

There is No Love in Control

You Cannot Control or Create Love

It is critical to understand that love is beyond the human mind. It cannot be thought. The human mind believes it is the source of our sense of love, and it can therefore orchestrate love. But it cannot. If you take nothing else from this book, please take that concept forth. It is liberating as it releases you from the naïve thought that we need to consciously chase love to bring it into existence.

Consciously seeking anything is a needy energy and contrary to the forces of love. Love responds to desire and flourishes in the energy of want and passion, not need. Resist this, and love will persist in giving you 'wake up calls' to redirect you back to its divine path. And these wake-up calls can be very confronting at times.

Trust is the key. You can allow yourself to be open to love and you can take your heart out into the world to feel its presence. However, you must trust that whether you find a frequency match or not at any given time is at the behest of the universe, and not your will. This is why chasing love usually only invites disappointment into your life – because in that instance your ego is your determiner of the presence of love.

Only your heart can know love when it arrives in your presence – so try less, relax more, have fun and let love enter your life when you are ready to truly receive it. Yes, this can be easier said than done, particularly if you have been single for a while, because we are so used to living primarily from our minds. But thinking love is a zero-sum gain, a fallacy, manipulated by many in the world for personal gain.

You cannot fall in love with someone because you want to, or don't want to. It is a natural phenomenon that is bestowed upon you by the orchestrating forces of two souls. All we can do is be open to love gracing our path as we do other things. But this is different to doing things to create love.

On several occasions I persisted in relationships, naïvely thinking that I might fall in love with another person if I gave it enough time, or we went on some great dates.

All I achieved was more romantic experiences, familiarity and a deeper connection on a human level. But what I could never do by trying hard, was to establish love. Only my soul could do that.

Many of us think that romance is love or can create love. Romantic experiences can feel great, but unless love is present these beautiful experiences are likely to only result in a temporary lift in our happiness. Romance is not love.

Love will often come along when you least expect it. Like many of the great experiences in life they are derived from spontaneity and synchronicity, the latter being the handy work of the universe. How people do you know who met their perfect match when they weren't looking? A loving vibrational match will arise when it is meant to, not when you hope it will.

Sometimes we need to feel loved, so we talk ourselves into the belief that we 'must be in love', or we use attraction or admiration as a poor surrogate for love, which it can never be.

Instead, the answer is to simply set the intention for love to grace your path. Think about the qualities that you want a loving partner to have, then develop your attractiveness to a potential match through the way you dress, the way you present yourself, the personality traits you portray and the level of success you project. These all relate to the bottom of the infinity symbol in Chapter 3's Figure 2 – our Earth-bound human side – and we can influence these.

I say 'influence' because we can't fully control these either. We all have our own sense of what we are attracted to, and others may or may not be attracted to our personal qualities or looks.

It's important, though, to remain true and authentic to yourself in any projection of yourself. You can present an image, but if it's not real you could enter a relationship under false pretences that you cannot sustain. That is unfair on you and any prospective partner and will make any relationship fragile.

I had the experience of asking out a woman I was deeply attracted to, only to witness her select a man who was the opposite of me in many ways. It was not easy, but I understood it completely and had to accept it.

He was well-known, younger and more sought-after than I was. I had to accept that the polarity between her and I was just not present for her, even if my heart felt deeply connected to hers.

When you are in an existing relationship, keeping the attraction flowing between you both is also important. Love may or may not be present, but effort to keep the sparks burning does matter. If we let the polarity fade, a relationship can atrophy, even if we still love the person. Try conscious relating to assist with building attraction and nourishing love with another, through allowing you to share your true feelings about your needs and desires.

The same is of course true at the start of a relationship, whenever it occurs. And that unknown can be a very positive experience too – since you can't control love, and you never know when it's going to appear, this introduces an element of excitement and mystery into your life, particularly if you are single.

How exciting and liberating is that!

Love Gets Overruled by Conditioning

If you had the choice, would you choose to live from the energy of fear or love? Love is fearless and adventurist. Whereas fear likes safety and security, and therefore repetition. When we experience the energy of love we can feel how much it expands our sense of appreciation of life. Our days just feel sunnier. When we experience the energy of fear, life can seem limited and restricted. The days can just drag.

So why not choose love? The choice *is* yours after all!

We might struggle to choose love because humanity has learned to put rules around love. We're all conditioned to want the fairytale, to need a romantic partner who meets the image created by our minds and the minds of the people we seek to impress – like family and friends, or in some rare cases where people are highly visible to society, the general masses.

Often, we want to be with the partner who expands our egoic perception of self, though that person may not match our heart's actual desires. It's our need for love pouring forth in a mental construct or checklist.

In my book *Where Your Happiness Hides*, I outline the dangers of living from what I call 'checklist love' – the art of predetermining the qualities of the person we seek to love and focussing our attention on meeting those mental constructs.

Unfortunately, love does not operate this way and couldn't care less about our mental constructs. It just is, regardless of the external qualities or possessions of another. Love does not seek to match itself with the external attributes of another person, for it simply can't. It is a high frequency, and won't match with something denser, like a Ferrari.

If we think that somebody's job, car, wealth, achievements, religion or social standing make them more lovable to our hearts, we are sadly mistaken. It may make them more attractive, and this does matter to a lot of people, but all is a choice and, ideally, we should all want to have a partner who ticks both the attraction and love boxes simultaneously.

Consider the American paradigm of love portrayed in so many adolescent movies. The quarter-back football star gets the most beautiful cheerleader, and they go on to be the prom queen and prom king. Amazing coincidence that love has brought two such perfect specimens together!

Of course when we 'fall in love' with an idea like this, we are playing by the rules of someone else's game – society's game.

Relationships based on attraction can work, but unlike love connections they are more prone to wane and diminish if the external qualities of another shift in some way, usually away from our preferred model of who we think our partner should be.

For example, if our preferred partner loses their job, income or puts on too much weight, they may be judged as less appealing by our minds. In this situation we may think that we have fallen out of love, but the attraction element of the relationship has simply diminished. Any love present has not changed. Our perception of its purity has merely been corrupted by our thoughts.

Most often, we are the only barrier to a union based on love, because either our lack of self-worth or perhaps our excessive self-worth blocks what is possible with mental constructs.

What if we consciously worked on those conditioned mental constructs and nullified them, letting love set the tone and the pathway forward? How liberating could that be?

It's just a choice, like all else in life, and perhaps the one thing we can control about our relationship with love itself.

Be the Conduit of Love, not its Container

Love is an energy, and it creates great emotions within us all. It therefore flows through all aspects of us. We truly can't contain it, nor will it let us. Try and contain it at your own risk!

Like all emotions, love is an energy that demands to be in motion. It seeks expression in many ways, including passionate love making.

Our role is to feel it and surrender to its gifts, for it is the source of all true passion.

We can try and think passion, but this is a falsehood. It must be felt.

We are truly a conduit for love, and when we think we own it, or that we should tone it down, we limit its power to create wonder in our lives.

Conduct it without resistance and it will light up your life, like a light globe waiting to be switched on.

The Serious Relationship Anomaly

If you ever go into a dating site, the system will often ask you if you are looking for a serious relationship or not.

Collectively we have become conditioned to think that 'serious' is better than 'fun' in life.

If someone loves me enough to marry me, then we will settle down and 'get serious'. Then we can perhaps take part in co-suffering!

The truth about love is that it is not serious, so why do we think that we must become serious with the person we love?

Love has a playful and fun energy, like a child looking at the world with wonder. It cares less about worry and seeks joy and fulfilment as its primary desires. It does not embrace suffering and knows infinite ways to avoid it.

Love is blissful, happy, light, curious, caring, compassionate and carries many other great qualities. But it is never serious. It loves life, not being tied down by our mental images of what it should look like. It is spontaneous and fresh in the moment, for it is pure presence and always in the now.

Whenever someone asks me if I'm looking for a serious relationship, I always say 'no, I'm looking for one that is fun and happy'. Then I observe their confused look. It goes against their conditioning about serious romantic relationships!

The real positive here is that, when we release the mirage that a great love match must create a serious relationship, we are free to let love takes us where it wants us to go.

And from here, there are no limits to what we can achieve in terms of joy in a loving union.

Becoming Owned by What You Want to Own

Our minds can very easily enter a loop of despair when they don't get what they want. This is where obsessions are formed. And obsessions normally result in regressions, for the freedom to choose is lost.

Obsessions always come from our personalities or egos, and not our hearts. Love does not obsess. Obsessing over someone we desire can be a great drain on our psyches and limit the level of love we are able to direct for the rest of our lives. It can be very distracting and take us out of presence.

Say we find a deep or profound connection with another soul, but that person rejects your interest in them, based on their own personal preferences? *Love* accepts this choice and can move into the energy of peace. Love will never force itself onto another, for it knows at a vibrational level that the other person is either not yet a match for their inherent frequency of love, or that they have just exercised their free will, which is the right of all. Love will thus accept and be at peace, not obsess over what could have been.

Our own acceptance is the price we must pay when we are rejected in the presence of deep love. The opportunity we are being given is to work through any residual pain that comes our way, for that pain allows us to cleanse our energies – it's not the other person's job to clear our pain. After all they can't even feel it!

Beware when rejection sets off a loop of conditioned or obsessive thinking that ultimately sees you engulfed and transfixed on the person you desired. You wanted to be admired and loved by them, all you got was unrequited love, and now you have to admit that you have become owned by your own obsessive thoughts and feelings. This can be hard to let go of, but let go we must.

Eventually you will come to see that the pain and the need to let go of your obsession with another is a path to a stronger, wiser you, and this is a gift from love.

This letting go process entails processing your pain as best you can. We must face the egoic feelings of despair and sadness, and process them one at a time as they arise into our hearts.

We might find that our minds create stories and emotions of despair as we enter a victim mentality through our repeated stories of rejection. And most likely our disappointments will be met by stories of being let down. But it's in these stories that we can find the golden nuggets of wisdom that we need to investigate further.

When we are rejected, any chinks in our self-worth can be exposed, and this is where we need to direct our attention and intentions. This is where 'gold' can be found – not in trying to control the experience, but in letting go of that control.

We should not give up on love, but we ideally need to let go of our expectations in the current circumstances. Giving up on love should never be an option.

The Kingdom of Love

Living from a place of love means being ruled by your heart, not by your ego, and herein lies a core issue for humanity.

Love demands equality. In the kingdom of love there is no control, no power over another, and no judgement, other than what might be expressed for the common good. We are one.

Love respects the role of your body and your mind, for its consciousness brought them forth. It knows that, without them, its current incarnation must end. It embraces this wholeness as nature at work.

In all relationships, love thus stands steadfastly for equality. There is no one person in-charge and no human king or queen sitting in judgement on another. There is harmony, free will, awareness and connection, and these energies orchestrate creativity.

Energy flows equally between all parties (unless there is a temporary need for it to do otherwise). There is balance. All involved in the relationship have the freedom to feel and express, for they are empowered by the love that arises from within them, not the need to conquer. Worship is no more.

There are no rules for the commoners to apply, other than those agreed upon by all, for love is the rule.

There are no 'tower moments' either, for love is relaxed, composed, humble and understands that all takes place for purpose. It approaches all hardships with curiosity and wonder, not worry.

The intelligence of love needs no swords or shields, for it has no fear. Conflict is replaced by compassion and care.

Love's kingdom is where real majesty lies.

You can create a true kingdom of love with someone you cherish if you can learn to interact together in a conscious way, with love leading the way, not your egos. Or you can do it for yourself.

Ascending the Steps to Love

If each relationship in life is a mirror that gives you the opportunity to grow through the power of love, and romantic relationships provide the most potent opportunities to grow, then each romantic relationship is also a step ascending towards true love within us, and with others. During each romantic encounter, you may therefore be heavily challenged to learn more about your true nature and remove your limiting beliefs and energies.

The diagram below shows pictorially how relationships can work as steps in this way. A person could also take each of these steps within a single relationship, which I'll therefore refer to as 'experiences':

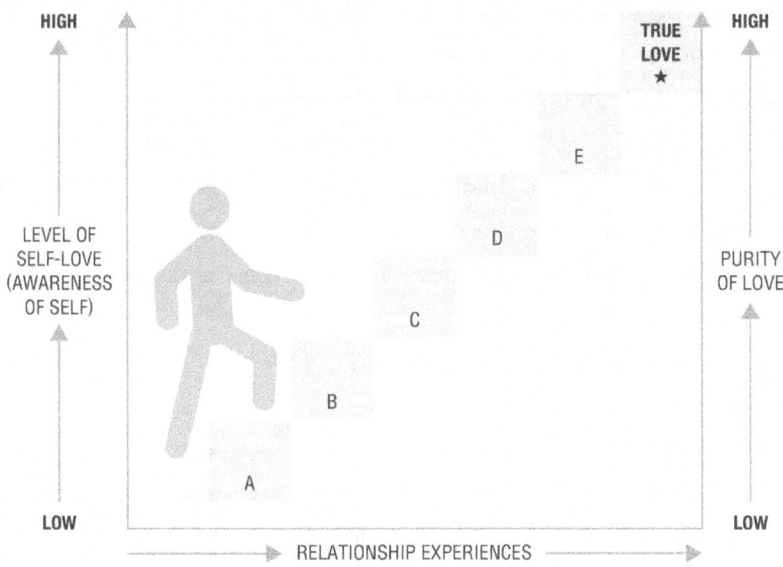

Figure 3: The Stairway to True Love

As we learn from each relationship experience, our potential to love without egoic distortions expands, and doing so with integrity creates a self-fulfilling prophecy of higher understandings. Each time we learn and become more in sync with love, either alone or with another, our personal vibration rises. And with every lift comes the opportunity to take your romantic and other relationships to a whole new level.

The level of self-love that a person can achieve (i.e. the higher up the staircase they can climb) then impacts the purity of love that they can also attain (essentially offer themselves), through giving to and receiving from those they love. And their self-love is primarily a product of their conditioned minds and karmic energies, for these illusions corrupt their ability to express love unconditionally, which just shows how important it is to clear your illusions.

Equally important as we climb through these steps is to continually love in the now. As this book explains, love is always found in presence. It therefore wants us to create our lives from the present moment. We can choose to live in the past or in a fictitious future, and not let go of past pains and dysfunctions that we experience, or we can rechoose our lives in every single moment that unfolds. This is love's preference, and it will guide the way, if we surrender to its infinite wisdom.

Our natural way is to process pain as it arises, to let it go and never give up on experiencing the wonders of love in our lives. When we learn to accept that the pain of separation or dislocation in relationships is a great teacher that helps us to evolve to another level, we can witness the steps in love's master plans, as they unfold in front of our very eyes. Illusion is the only enemy of love.

When we think that the past must repeat itself, and we become 'twice shy', we can shield ourselves from the new possibilities that we so richly deserve.

So, even though it's easier said than done, we need to choose to love in the now, not in the past or the future, for love only ever operates in this way.

It's a bit like climbing a mountain and arriving at a peak with a spectacular view you've never witnessed before. You could not see the view until you got to the summit, but you had to do the hard yards to get there first.

Ideally, if we grow in love with our current partner, our existing relationships can serve us well on our path to higher awareness and more intense levels of love.

However, if our current relationships do not meet this need, they are likely to end at the hands of love itself. The primary thing from a universal perspective is that you grow closer to your own heart. The universe is patient, but it won't stand idle and watch you stagnate forever.

Like the river analogy earlier, new energies will invariably enter your life to allow you to flow forwards, and sometimes you will have no resistance to these new events and truths that come calling.

If you do grow as intended, the next loving relationship you experience will meet you in your higher level of frequency. In other words, as you expand and arise, so will the potentialities of the relationships that you experience next.

Don't learn your lessons, on the other hand, and you will be forced to repeat the classes that you failed.

So, although it's hard to hear, each relationship that ends could be a step-up to an even better one for you. It all depends on how much you learn along the way.

Conscious relating can allow you to enter a more advanced romantic relationship without the costs and pain of starting again.

I recommend that you consider this magical formula closely for relationship harmony!

The steps that apply to external relationships also apply to individuals in isolation. If you are single or on the path to higher self-awareness alone, every lift you achieve, even alone, brings you closer to your true self and the true love you can feel within yourself.

Conscious relating can be done alone or with another, but either way it is a gift you can give yourself.

Choose How You Make Choices

Life is determined by the series of choices that you make.

Unless our freedoms are unfairly taken away from us, we have free-will on the Earth to choose our own actions and make our own decisions. You can choose your path.

But where you choose from is the important thing that influences your quality of life. We can choose from a place of ignorance or intelligence.

Love is connected to pure intelligence and your heart always knows what will best serve your future. It also knows with whom you are meant to have loving relationships. If we make decisions from our egoic minds alone, and not from our loving hearts, we can risk making choices that are out of step with what will bring us the greatest happiness and growth.

What does this mean for romantic love? It means choosing with your heart and mind in concert. All decisions are always best made from the profound combination of love and logic. This is what it means to be integrated, or to be in integrity – it means to have your heart, mind and body all in sync. It doesn't just mean saying or doing what you think is right, because thought is a mental construct that you can control, it is not love. Instead, we must value ourselves completely.

When you are 'in integrity' in this way, you are in the energy of truth on all levels. Your heart, body and mind are all aligned in the energy of love. You feel, think and act from the energy of love, for here lies truth.

If a person finds it hard to feel into their body or heart, it will not be easy for them to access their truths, for feelings are the gateway to integrity. This is why it's so important to feel, then act, from the energy of love.

Try to feel your decisions before you try to think them. If the heart, mind and body are all involved in a decision, then the combined power of love and logic will escort you to a place of true integrity.

Choosing a loving partner is no different. Love and logic must play their combined parts in the process of creating union. While your heart can detect the presence of love, your mind and body can assess your level of attraction to another.

Why would anyone not consult both aspects of their intelligence? To do otherwise would mean you are choosing from a place of partial ignorance, without all the cards in your hand!

There can be much pain if you are choosing a partner without full awareness.

Stress and a lack of peace have befallen me when I have chosen to chase attraction, rather than the purity of the love I crave. I now refuse to do it and would prefer to be single than in a mediocre love match.

Conversely, if your heart, body and mind are all aligned in the energy of love, and in that place you match with another whose heart, body and mind are all aligned in the energy of love – can you imagine how powerful that relationship would be? To meet someone and be drawn to them on all three levels would be a wonderful thing and probably akin to nirvana for those who enter such a relationship.

Perhaps some readers have had this magical experience?

PART B

The Endless Human Cycle from Separation Back to Union

CHAPTER 6

Untold Truths About Separation

Separation is a Core Belief

A true nuance of life on Earth is that your inner reality will always reflect out into your outside circumstances. This arises because of vibrational resonance, or the law of attraction. We always attract into our lives the equivalent of our own vibrational resonance, being a function of our core energies and beliefs.

For example, if we believe that we deserve to suffer, consciously or subconsciously, we will attract that energy towards us – that is the way life on Earth works. As Isaac Newton's third law of physics states: every reaction always has an equal and opposite reaction. It's all just frequency at work.

Ironically, we think that we can keep secrets and thoughts in our own mind, and they will never be known to another. This may be true of other people's minds, but our souls and the souls of others are in full awareness, even of your thoughts! The universe knows exactly what you are thinking, and your soul is always ready to create circumstances and synchronicities to bring you closer to your true self.

There is complete awareness of all things in the metaphysical realms, but not on this planet, for we generally live from our rudimentary brains.

So, what does this mean for those with separation as a core belief?

As human beings, we all fundamentally believe in separation. We have been taught that we are all beings living on this planet in separation, that it is essentially every man and woman for themselves, with some semblance of family and community connection.

This is because, when we are born onto the Earth, we are intentionally given amnesia, preventing most of us from being aware of what we are and where we have come from – our souls chose this challenge for us, wanting us to take on the task of rediscovering our truth as universal beings and coming home to our true selves.

As we grow up, we then absorb and accept the normal misconception that we are all separate from each other and from the rest of the universe. It normally takes wise parents to prevent this belief from taking root within our psyches.

At its ultimate projection, many of us are taught, by word or assumption, that we are alone in the universe, and that God has abandoned us, and sent us to die on this rock in space. Essentially, we doubt our eternal realities, for we are not collectively sure of this truth.

Is it any wonder that separation consciousness is the typical state of understanding on Earth? And that this ignorance leads us to an overarching belief in the inevitability of separation, which we then project and attract?

When separation is our normal mindset, of course the lives that we create can't help but be full of circumstances that reflect this core and common belief structure!

But for union and reunion to become the key inspiration we believe in and live by, we need to move to unity consciousness as our accepted state of awareness, and we need to do the inner work needed to bring our hearts, minds, bodies and spiritual energies into alignment, such that together they are natural in their expression with each other.

Union must start within us first, so that it can ripple out into the world that we inhabit.

But instead of understanding that any relationship issues we are experiencing have been being brought forth for both parties to learn more about themselves, and to grow through the issues being manifested, we often walk away or quit without due effort to resolve the problems. This arises because separation is our conditioned mindset, and we are ignorant of the gift that relationship challenges represent, being a kind of magic mirror held up for both parties to witness their own inner truths. Instead we smash the mirror to protect our egos from blame!

If we were more aware of and listened to our loving hearts, they would always urge us to take a more constructive path to knowing ourselves more fully and investigate with wonder what the magic mirror can reflect within us, for us to see.

Separation will, however, continue to haunt us, one relationship at a time, the world over, until enough people understand that relationships give us all the opportunity to grow individually and together.

This doesn't mean that separations between lovers won't occur even in full awareness, but more couples are likely to see their differences as opportunities for higher awareness and will be able to work through their differences in a far more constructive way.

And if they still choose to separate, they are likely to end in a higher degree of appreciation for each other, and gratitude for the time both partners spent together.

Increased awareness – that love creates challenges for us and through us for our own benefit, rather than to harm us – would improve our world immensely. Difficulties are essentially a test, and many loving relationships are tests on steroids, for they do give us great highs and lows.

Look Ahead!

When I was trying to come to terms with my own previous separations, I found it useful to reflect on the lyrics of the song 'Defying Gravity' from the stage-play Wicked. In it, a persona realises they've been afraid of losing love for too long, feeling that the cost of losing love was too great, yet seeing that they deserved better than the love they were attracting into their lives.

It reminded me that I had been guilty of being desperate to hold onto some romantic relationships, even if the other person was no longer able to value me. And in this process of hanging on for too long, I had failed to value myself.

Conscious relating was not a skill I had any knowledge of in my early relationships. And neither did some of my partners. As a result, issues we faced were not dealt with well, and tended to go unresolved because of the absence of truth.

I also did not understand that sometimes relationships run their course and may need to end for the good of both parties, in different ways.

Sometimes we need to let go of something to let in something better! And better may mean a person of a higher frequency match that your heart, or your partner's heart, knows is on its way.

Both parties will always be able to learn from the separation experience if they feel into their emotions, so the cost is surely worthwhile from a learning perspective.

Eventually, I did of course learn, in every case, though it was often too late to avoid pain. I did most of my detailed self-reflection after relationships had ended, when I started to understand the path to higher awareness.

For example, I was initially devastated when my second marriage ended, but eventually saw the purpose of the split. I grew more through that separation than through any other event in my life.

I was finally awoken to the truth of my own self-love by pain. Self-respect descended on my life at a level I never known before. This took a lot of soul-searching, but it was so valuable to my well-being.

As the song 'Defying Gravity' points out, the energetic cost of staying in a relationship that no longer serves either party is sometimes too high to bear. And your heart knows when the costs are no longer in your best interests to endure.

Listening to your heart is the key. There can be great pain in a breakup, but this pain holds great wisdom, and once heard and learned from, this pain will pass, leaving you refreshed and ready for the next opportunity to love.

Self-love is critical and must be put above your love for another in romance. But this is often not what we have been taught.

Popular Plots, Joining the Dots!

Don't just trust in my experience of course, trust in your own! Let's look at the stories you watch on your television or at the cinema. You know the ones – boy meets girl and both fall in love. Cupid's arrow strikes their hearts. However, somewhere along the way, tragedy or unfortunate circumstances force the lovers apart. Confusion and tension grip the viewer as the disappointment reminds them of their own misadventures of love.

But wait! Fate has a different plan, the one our hearts were hoping to see! After a series of uncanny moments of synchronicity and the unexpected disclosure of true feelings, the two lovers realise they must be together after all!

Feeling overcomes thought. True love is present. The happily-ever-after happens once again, and we love it! Romance fills our screens and leaves us feeling joy in our hearts. We return to our lives deep in personal reflection, or holding our own lover that little bit tighter, dreaming of our own happily-ever-after.

But this story is not confined to our cinema or television screens – it is the story of life on Earth, and it plays out in every walk of life: business, between nations, within families, and through communities far and wide. There are many stories and plots that unfold for us every day in this world, where we each have our own unique cast with whom we are interacting. Love is ultimately the director, cast, crew and audience that brings our movies to our screens!

We have free will, of course, as to how we will influence the story of our own lives; but the underlying question remains: will we choose the scenes from intelligence or ignorance, from love or fear? For that choice is critical to our experiences!

The separations we see in the movies are often unavoidable in real life too, yet they can be embraced and learned from for our own sense of self. We can harness them for our own self-knowing, should we choose to do so, whether they are merely temporary or remain permanent. Regardless of the outcome, you can learn much about yourself if you surrender to love's lessons.

Like a long-running Shakespeare tale, the story of separation and its relationship with reunion is a play that we can all bring to a fitting finale, or at least a more pleasant ending, once we know how.

The curtain can fall, and we can all take a bow once our conscious awareness is high enough to support it and construct a different script, rich in union and love.

Separations will still occur, but how we handle them will be different. We can embrace them in the energy of empathy and compassion for all.

Until we learn to do so, our lives are likely to be punctuated by loss and full of the blame game. Occasional happiness will never revert to the bliss we were born to enjoy until we can end this nagging cycle of self-destruction, because harmonious union demands intelligence, not ignorance – and that intelligence is already inside you for you are it. You are love.

A Biblical Story of Separation

We have all heard of the Garden of Eden.

It is written into the Bible's book of Genesis and depicted as a terrestrial paradise where the first man and woman, Adam and Eve, lived in bliss on Earth.

Now, I am not religious. However, I believe this story has deep significance to the dance between lovers and illustrates the story of separation in our psyches.

The Garden of Eden was recorded as a sacred place, which provided divinely for those who lived there. Adam and Eve had the ability to live there forever. They were free to eat from any tree in the garden, except for the forbidden fruit grown by the tree of knowledge of good and evil.

The story tells us that a serpent seduced Adam and Eve and convinced them to eat from the sacred tree of knowledge.

Both were then expelled from the garden, and legend says they were deprived of their ability to live forever. They had sinned and paid the ultimate price.

This story has deep significance for humanity, since in separating from their paradise, Adam and Eve were separated from God – from the ultimate source of love. The story is thus one of separation and abandonment.

But is it possible for Adam and Eve, and those who came in the generations that followed, to return to this garden in beautiful union and remember the paradise that was lost?

The answer is YES!

Returning home to unconditional love is possible for us all. The garden represents our version of heaven on Earth, rich in love. Access to this garden is our birthright to reclaim. And in this place love is the dominant force.

We just need to know how to open the gate that we 'think' is currently in our way and stopping us from accessing this magical place.

But here is the catch – the truth is that we never truly left this garden of purity, and neither did Adam and Eve.

And the gate that I refer to is not real. It is no more than a barrier steeped in love and created by our human conditioning and imaginations.

We just believed that we had been separated from the garden and from our sacred home, full of love.

Only our illusions have kept us from enjoying the bliss that our gardens and their inherent foundations of love allow, within ourselves and with our lovers.

The journey from separation, through isolation and back into the reunification within our garden, awaits us, and is in fact our destiny.

Only ignorance keeps us on the other side of the gate.

And this seemingly endless process, from separation back to union, is so ingrained in the history of our romantic experiences.

Reunion is inevitable, when we are ready to move through our self-imposed gates and recreate heaven on Earth. It is just a choice; be it is a hard choice to make from the energies of a conditioned mind.

Our human obsession with separation and reunion, reflects the separation that exists within us between our minds, bodies and hearts.

Our story is a tragedy and a love story all rolled into one, yet it's a story many of us have distorted in our belief that we need to keep proving to the world that we are worthy of love.

But when we are ready to see the truth of love, we can all return home to our absolute selves, and come into beautiful unions with others.

Learning From the Aggregation of the Pain of Separation

Separation and the disappointment that arises within us can be extremely painful.

Lost loves and rejection have been without doubt the most haunting experiences of my own life. It took me years to overcome the loss of my deepest loves.

And these painful experiences can aggregate over time and destroy your faith in both love and YOU.

Stopping this aggregation of pain is critical to our happiness and mental health. Understanding that separation has happened for you, and not to you, can start the process of releasing this haunting pain.

I hope that others will come to see what I have been taught and release themselves from the prison of despair that rejection has probably locked them into. The key to those locks lies in the wisdom that love wants you to know yourself as love and be in union with your own heart, so you can never, ever be rejected again.

Separation need not even be the case between people in conflict or misalignment. Deep self-reflection, if properly undertaken, can allow one or both parties to transform their energy, reinstating the strength of the bond they share. This relies upon high levels of self-awareness; a gift many have not yet been taught to attain. But it is possible.

Whereas, when our egos take us out of the energy of love, our relationships are all at risk of ending prematurely, even when all they were doing was helping us to grow together.

Of course, we must also face the reality that many relationships are not meant to last forever. This is often not what our conditioned minds find acceptable, and this leads us away from peace and harmony when a relationship reaches its end point. But the universe uses relationships to teach us more, and more, about ourselves, so inevitably once we have learned what we needed to learn from such relationships, we may find ourselves in a frequency mismatch that ends them.

Love is, after all, an ever-changing river, not a serene pond of tranquil waters. Once we realise this, we can experience love's many highs and lows with composure and compassion. This doesn't mean to say we won't still experience pain when relationships end, but they are more likely to bring us into greater wholeness within ourselves, leaving us in the energy of gratitude for the relationship – for the universe never makes mistakes.

And when we can apply compassion and gratitude to ourselves and others when a relationship ends, rather than look for blame and shame, we can bring forth the true intent of the relationship issues and allow new relationships of a higher vibration to follow.

Over nine relationships that ended in separation, I was able to clearly see what I was meant to see in this life about my greatest nemeses: romantic relationships and intimacy.

I was originally self-deprecating about my relationship track-

record, but in hindsight I now see how much about myself I truly needed to see, and thankfully have.

My Romantic Relationship Lessons

After a series of romantic relationships, I did some deep self-enquiry as to what I needed to learn. And my lessons were profound.

Essentially, my self-worth was too low, and this led me to think the following limiting ways about myself – they might sound familiar to you too:

- *I am not enough and not truly lovable*
- *I am not worthy of very beautiful women*
- *There are other men who are more worthy than I, particularly younger richer and more successful ones*
- *The more money I make and the richer I get, the more a woman can love me*
- *To make sure a woman loves me, I must give her whatever she asks for – what she gives me back matters less, because if she leaves, I may never find love again*
- *I don't matter as much as she does, for I need to be loved*
- *I am more worthy if I have a partner I love*
- *Being in the presence of a beautiful woman validates me, particularly if she will be sexual or intimate with me*
- *My job is to work hard to make sure she has all the material things that she wants, so that I am safe too*

This cocktail of limiting beliefs led me to focus too much on work and money in relationships, as I essentially tried to buy love from someone I loved! I tried to buy something that I already was and could have offered myself for free!

My level of success, I thought, was the main determiner of my lovability and attractiveness as a romantic partner.

It did not help that, at the age of 21, I was told by my mother that I should never expect to be loved by a woman whose family has more money than my own. Unfortunately, my subconscious mind believed her!

My lack of skill and self-esteem in relationships clearly played out in the end to my detriment. Because I did not love myself enough. I lost faith in love itself.

I wanted to be the saviour of someone beautiful, and their knight in shining armour, who would save them from the wicked witch and the tower within which they were suffering. And so they would be forever in my debt, never wanting to leave my side.

Too many fairytales had led me to a fantasy I would never find. In fact, I got the opposite.

Separation was my great fear, so guess what my vibration brought forth?

I gave too much money and not enough love to my partners at times. And when I met or dated women who did not validate me the way I expected them to, I was less inclined to be interested in them.

My inner reality became my outer experience, for I believe I walked away from some beautiful women who loved me. I essentially, self-destructed.

My heart clearly wanted me to have these lessons and magnetised me to women who would allow the right lessons to unfold.

Losing my two marriages cost me a lot of the very things I thought made me attractive and lovable, like my wealth. But I now see that this was love's master plan.

In the end, I paid lots of money for great learnings, and my soul is glad that I did for now I see that I was lovable all the time.

My ego just did not believe it.

Separations Get Faster and Harder

One of the quirks of love is that, if you do not learn its lessons effectively enough, it will bring you the same lessons that you failed to learn from, faster and harder each time.

If you experience a lesson, it is because your soul knows that you are ready to face that lesson. You will never receive a lesson that you cannot truly cope with.

This is another comforting way of viewing a difficult life. It normally means that you are an advanced soul, taking on advanced lessons.

Equally, once you learn thoroughly from a lesson, it will not be brought into your periphery again, for you have essentially passed that test.

This is why it is so important to learn from life's experiences as they unfold, rather than just blame another, or put them down as bad luck and try again from the same level of awareness that contributed to the previous problems. Luck is a misnomer in relationships. It may apply to lotto, but not your marriage!

Education on Separation

It would be wonderful if our children could be taught the truth about union and shown that separations can be viewed constructively, and even avoided with a higher level of conscious awareness.

Perhaps this book can help in that regard?

It is time we stopped seeing relationship problems and even separations as evil.

They are rife in all aspects of our lives, so learning to honour and value them as learning opportunities and upward steps to a wiser you, could make them a divine experience, and turn the pain they hold into great personal power.

If you ultimately want true love to grace your path, these are the steps you must embrace.

PART C

HUMAN PARADIGMS OF LOVE

CHAPTER 7

Popular Paradigms of Love

The Never-Ending Quest for True Love

Most humans dream of finding true love in their lives, and the phrase 'true love' is used repeatedly in society. But do we really know what it is and how to attain it? The answer is a resounding, 'no!'.

True love is another way of referring to unconditional love, and this kind of love between two people is extremely rare. That's the bad news. We may think we have it, but the truth is we probably don't. It is the ultimate level in love, within us and with another.

But that doesn't mean we can't work towards it, because we can. And that's the good news. It is a natural state we can all attain.

To attain true love, two people must essentially be aligned with their true selves and unconditionally love themselves. In other words, both must be living from their hearts and be in their light. They are largely free of limited beliefs and negative energies.

Removing all barriers to become your true self is one of the greatest accomplishments that any human being can attain, though from my experience it takes a strong commitment to living a highly conscious life, and this is not normal.

The wisdom of how to do this has also been largely lost in the annals of time, unfortunately. My teachings on this subject have been vast and are encapsulated in my book *From Pain to Possibility*.

In a world that is constantly trying to teach you who you need to be, to be successful, is it any wonder that we find it hard to break through our conditioned mindsets and thoughts? Of course, because this can be such a hard path to take! And who wants to do the hard work on their own self-awareness when there is an easier and less challenging path that can be followed?

Many people will do the hard work to make money or progress in their career, but it's not normal to do the hard yards to establish greater self-awareness, or to use that greater self-awareness to enhance a loving relationship. The more you know about you, the more you can become, and the more your romantic relationship can also become. Why not be the becoming of you?

Accordingly, very few people in one incarnation will discover their true selves and demolish their limited belief structures. Even less will take on their karma from past lives or do their work to cleanse their energy fields, like I have done.

But who would even do this if they do not first understand that it is possible, and completely natural.

In the rare event that two people find their own pure self-love and the light that emanates from their true selves, true love is possible. In this rare place there is no need, and all the wonderful qualities of love come to the fore, in and through their relationship.

Two lovers in the energy of unconditional love need nothing from anyone else, or each other, and this experience is one in which showers of love overflow onto each other. Both parties will give and receive love in equal measures for both participants are sharing their pure frequencies, willingly. Both lovers are free of judgements, demands, impatience and expectations. Compassion and care for each other are plentiful. The purity of passion abounds, because both lovers are mutually engaged in the relationship for each other, with each other and as each other.

They are 'as each other' for they both know that they are equal and of the same loving vibration. They are one, vibrationally. The union is complete and love alone drives the relationship forward, devoid of limitations and full of endless possibilities. Both lovers know that judgement is ignorance, not intelligence, so they replace judgement with understanding and compassion.

True love is the ultimate loving relationship between two souls and is often the domain of high-level soul mates and twin flames. Such relationships are secure and can be unbreakable, not because of the existence of a promise or contract like marriage, but because both lovers know in their hearts that this is the purity they desired in love.

They no longer question whether their relationship is right for them. There is an inherent knowing that this is as good as it gets. And a sense of peace is present, when they are together.

Such relationships can take many lifetimes to bring into fruition, for a vibrational match at this high frequency is extremely advanced.

Many of us can create relationships at high levels of purity, but true love is at a level that few will experience in this lifetime.

But it is possible if someone fully commits to the path of discovering their true selves, and this to me was an exciting adventure I really wanted to take.

Perhaps you will too.

Current energies on the Earth are lifting making this opportunity for true love increasingly possible for those who are driven to 'achieve' it. But it will still take great commitment for most depending on their inherent frequencies and the extent of negative energies that need to be transmuted.

Although I speak of soul contracts and twin flames, chasing these concepts is not necessarily one you should pursue, unless it is of great interest to you. There are many advisers out there who claim that they can help you on this journey, but the way forward for us all is simple: just trust your heart to guide you into the next relationship that you are ready to experience. If you go chasing the ultimate relationship and true love before you are ready for it to unfold, you will miss the magic of the journey and just end up frustrated by your own situation.

Remember, the universe does not like need and will systematically dismantle it.

Just love when you love and feel your way forward.

Find and ignite the flame in your own heart, and the matching flame will be brought forth by the power of love in divine timing.

Not True But Still Great Love

If you are in a relationship that feels great, to some extent it doesn't matter what tag you put on it – true love or not.

If your heart is telling you that you are where you are meant to be, experiencing what you love with someone special, then you are most likely in the right relationship, growing in love.

In this situation you have a vibrational match that you should probably continue to enjoy and grow within.

But if you really want true love of the highest purity, you can also attain it – but it will involve an intense internal process first and foremost, raising your own frequency, rather than an externally focussed process of looking at the marketplace of prospective partners and impressing them with things that aren't even you.

You must find your own true love first, and then you can share it with another, who has also done the inner work to share this experience with you, or who is naturally highly self-aware. Some people just are!

True love is not given away easily by the universe. You must earn it.

True Love Doesn't Need to Be Romantic

When we think of true love, we usually think of it existing within a romantic relationship. However, true love can just as easily be expressed outside of a romantic partnership.

True love can be felt between family members and friendships, if egoic barriers do not distort the natural frequency of love being shared.

We often can have quite pure love connections with our family and friends because the negative mental constructs between individuals can be less intense, than they are with a romantic lover. However, they are prone to have less highs than intimate loving experiences.

You may also feel a powerful love connection with another person, but they may not want to share an intimate relationship with you. In this situation it is likely that one of the parties are not energetically ready to experience this extraordinary experience. Perhaps more growth is needed by one or both individuals.

A situation like this, may not feel like one full of love, but what if you needed the rejection, more than you needed an acceptance of your romantic interests, for your growth and development?

The soul knows what we need most, and it gives it to us out of pure love. This can be inside a partnership, or outside of one.

True Love is What You Are, Even Alone

When we speak of true love, we normally think of a romantic relationship between two people in a state of pure love. However true love is possible within each of us, whether we are single or attached, since we are all pure love at our core. And pure love is another word for true love!

When you take a conscious approach to your own life, you can move into an integrated state and become one with your own true love.

You do not need a partner to be in this energy of true love. In my book, *From Pain to Possibility*, I describe the natural path to the true self. Follow this approach and your own true love is yours for the taking. From there true love with another becomes even more possible.

I did most of my journey to self-love alone, with the occasional foray into the dating world. I found that my ability to face my truths was easier when I could do it privately. However, this depends on the level of openness and desire that your partner has to work with you on your respective growth opportunities.

The choice to find your own true love, alone or in tandem with another is just a choice.

True emotional intimacy can be attained quite quickly within yourself, rather than with another, when you learn to be 'into-my-self.'

Not a perfect match in words, I know, but you get my meaning.

Our Obsession With Fairytales

We grow up from a young and tender age being bombarded with fairy tales, in which the prince and princess live happily ever after. They are both gorgeous and their lives are perfect.

Our subconscious belief structures are primed from a young age to believe that we also deserve this fate, not as princes and princesses for they are rare, but as highly successful members of society.

These fairytales are based on a premise that love, once found, is forever and will not be anything but perfect.

Now, this might be the case in true love, but in most relationships, confronting moments will continually arise. Why? Because this is how love has defined and arranged them, so that relationships can be a vehicle to higher awareness, and not just partnerships for us to create a pleasant life from within.

Indeed, like it or not, the universe often pairs us with the right, wrong person to show us what we are not, and what we can become. Conflicts and disagreements will almost certainly arise in such relationships, because the wounds of both parties will be exposed through their interactions.

Such events can provide the opportunity for both parties to grow, but are likely to also put a strain on the relationship until the couple learns to consciously work through their wounds and grow together.

Differences between lovers may not be visible when two lovers initially come together and commit to each other, but the intent of the relationship will most likely bring them forth.

If those differences are not handled well enough, they may then break the relationship, because not every relationship is meant to have a fairytale ending, even if we want them to. It ultimately depends on the life plans of the individuals involved, and how we handle the challenges we encounter. This might be hard to hear for some, and a relief for others. We can try and resist the power of love, but this often results in pain and discomfort, which we will most likely endure, for we have stepped out of alignment with love and our soul's divine intentions.

Relationships will sometimes end because they simply must, so that we can have our next learning and higher vibrational, loving opportunity.

Our minds may struggle to witness the ending of a relationship as a chance for new beginnings, for they like to protect our often-fragile egos from pain. But knowing the true intent of relationships is important if we want to approach them in an advanced way.

We dream of meeting Mr or Mrs Right and staying together for the rest of our lives, unaware that what is right for us evolves, just like we do. We all seek certainty in our lives and resist change. But what if change is in our interests and supports our expansion back to true love?

Happily-ever-afters are not always on the agenda – until they are!

The Soul Mate Mythology

Like the concept of true love, a common misconception exists in society around the topic of soul mates.

A soul mate relationship is seen by many as the ultimate romantic relationship available to a human being. This is false.

We travel through life, lifetime after lifetime, with our soul family. These are souls that have chosen to help each other evolve upon the Earth. But there are typically many souls in these soul families, not just two.

Soul mates can take on different roles in our lives. In one life, a soul may play the role of your wife, and in the next life they may be your mother.

I use this example for it was one that applied to me.

Soul mates can evolve alongside us in multiple lives, and by virtue of that, when we meet one in the current life, we get a strong sense of remembering them. This energetic alignment is felt as love, but it can vary in intensity.

Some soul mate relationships can be very serene and loving, or they can be intense. It depends on their universal intent and the 'karmic history' of the two souls.

So, yes, we can be romantic with a soul mate in this life, but we may encounter multiple soul mates before we die. Some may provide us with romantic love and others may not.

There is, however, a being known as your twin flame that you can encounter in some lives. I say can, because you may not. Twin flames are our true and ultimate lovers, with whom we will often enjoy an unbreakable bond and true love. We all have one, but only one, and they journey through eternity with us – for they are us! We are the same consciousness, for we are of the same soul.

When a soul is created, there are believed to be two mirroring energies within that soul, like a ying and a yang. When they come together there is total consciousness of each other, for you are of the one consciousness, and the love between you can be complete.

When both twin flames are in their energy of pure love, the experience of coming together can be totally magnetising and passionate for there is no greater love that is possible on the Earth.

I speak more on this topic in my book *From Pain to Possibility*, and how what most of society refers to as a soul mate relationship is truly referring to a twin flame encounter or reunion.

Of course this may be seen as semantics, and of course it is best to just follow your heart and not get too caught up in the tags we can attach to our lovers. If you feel in love, just go for it, if you can.

But there are experts who offer advice on twin flame and soul-mate experiences. If you are ready to learn more you can contact me, or one of these other experts for advice. The internet is full of free articles on this subject.

More Modern Marriages

Marriage has been an institution in most societies for thousands of years, presented as a sign that two people intend to be in their relationship forever, as a contractual commitment intended to last for the rest of their lives.

To some people, marriage gives them a sense of added security and safety in their domestic lives. It gives many the foundation to bring new children into this world.

But if some relationships are not meant to be together forever, we may need to reassess the way we view marriages and divorces. As I have repeated purposely for emphasis, we come together with people for love and learning, then we often move on in search of our next loving experience, even though this can be shattering for some, particularly those who have been left by another.

We know this pain all too well. And we all too readily express blame and feel shame when our marriages end, because we feel abandoned and betrayed by our partner. Yet a more aware way of looking at breakups and divorces would be to accept that it is the natural endpoint of a successful experience together, then self-reflect over what can be learnt.

After my first marriage ended, it took me three months to admit it to some friends. I left the marriage, so I carried a heavy burden of guilt.

The pain of my second marriage ending, at my wife's request, was so overwhelming that it catapulted me into new levels of awareness that I could not have seen coming. It did involve a lengthy legal process, which was difficult and expensive for all involved.

But I soon attained great levels of gratitude for my marriage, because I took the time to see the learnings that my divorce brought into my life. I would not have received these learnings had the marriage not ended.

I am a strong supporter of marriage, despite my two divorces. I would only do it again if I felt deep love for my future wife and the purity of love I now know is possible. I am now capable of expressing a higher frequency of love and would also enter the marriage with my eyes wide open, such that if it ended it would not define me or impact on my self-esteem, like the last two did in different ways.

We don't need another to marry in truth. When you follow the path to self-love, you can find oneness within yourself. In this beautiful energy, your heart, mind and body are essentially married and unified by the force of love within you. This may bring solace to those who are single.

Contract or no contract, love has its own sovereignty to express, within you, then with another.

Other Non-Romantic Relationships

We build and explore many kinds of non-romantic relationships in our lives. These can be with family members, friends, work colleagues, and so on. The list is endless, because love is ever-present around us and is therefore behind every human interaction we experience, even our interactions with nature.

The frequency of love in these different types of relationships does vary, however. Let's start with families.

Most people have a family with whom they have grown up, and the love they feel within a family situation has a different feel to romantic love. It's still love, but these relationships have their own set of conditioned principles.

We are somewhat conditioned to believe that we must strongly love our other family members. But the same principles of frequency matching apply, and so some of us may not love our families as strongly as others.

That said, the bond between parent and child is typically very strong. They have chosen to share a life together at a soul level and do share common DNA. For a child to survive it typically learns to rely on its parents for support and nourishment. Even an adopted child who has never properly met their parents will crave to meet them, because of the bond of love and the power of curiosity that is always present.

However, the frequency of love between siblings and between other designated family members, like cousins, tends not to carry the same frequency of attachment. Accordingly, these types of relationships are more likely to shift and change, than our romantic and child/parent bonds.

Families can also change shapes, particularly when divorces or breakups take place, but regardless of this shape, love will always be present. It may not be felt, as it is less pure than before, but is still there.

Our conditioned mindsets about the various roles of family members and how we should interact are often cultural in nature. Respect your elders, be nice to your siblings, catch-up with your cousins, uncles and aunties, be nice to your mother-in law – any of these examples ring a bell?

The reality is that our desire to interact with different family members depends on the energetic relationships we share. We are often slaves to family structures that project us into a place of obligation, rather than want, when interacting with each other. But this does not need to happen. We can choose for ourselves.

The child parent bond may be largely unbreakable, but isn't it time we *decided* which family members we want to interact with and how this should take place? In many families, societal and family protocols and obligations tend to be the force that shapes these relationships rather than love itself. But the truth is that, in every life we are born into, we slot into a different family tree and have interactions with different ancestorial lines. This raises interesting questions about families and our heritages.

My past life enquiries have shown me that I have had many different lives in many different cultures and families. I may be Australian in this life, but in the 'past' I have been Samoan, Egyptian, English, French, Turkish, American and many more. These differing incarnations were the result of different choices made by my soul for its own experiences.

I no longer consider myself to be just Australian and part of my current family. I am a universal being having different lives as my soul sees fit. I am just a being, being human.

So, why obsess over family and/or cultural heritage when the reality is that we are likely to return repeatedly in different guises? We may long to belong to the group of people we call our family, but the truth is that we are all one big family no matter where we call home. Perhaps it's time the world respected this fact?

Our relationships with friends and colleagues are different again. We often struggle to say that we love our friends or colleagues, because that does not align with our conditioned mindsets around love. But we can decide to change that, as it can change with a simple mindset shift. Just because we will never be sexually intimate with a friend, or tell them all our life secrets, doesn't mean we can't love them and express that love in other ways.

Our many workplaces often feel devoid of love and create inherent competition between workers for the benefit of the bottom line. The flow of love between work colleagues would rarely be called that, even though it truly exists, and can be nurtured by the leaders.

The same goes in many community-based institutions, and in fact in society.

My book *Show Me the Harmony* explores what is possible in organisations that promote a loving culture rather than a fear-based one.

Isn't it time we opened ourselves up to the reality that the frequency of love exists between all human beings? It may vary in intensity in terms of the matches we feel and sexual forces, but our conditioned mindsets have blocked the flow of love across so many types of relationships we encounter, even country to country. We are now largely ignorant about the one big thing that we all desire to experience most and inherently are: love. Let's stop ignoring this incredible bond that all of humanity shares!

I'd love to see this level of awareness about the truth of love seep into our intelligences!

A movement from ignorance to intelligence is underway. The exciting prospect for every reader is that you can make a more conscious choice about how you interact with other people, including lovers, once you dismiss the need to meet certain normal paradigms of behaviour, and allow love (not obligations) to decide how you interact.

In this place, the sky is the limit.

CHAPTER 8

The Endless Dance of Masculine and Feminine Energies

What Dance Are We Doing Together?

Dancing is a good analogy for the special relationship that is expressed in romantic relationships between masculine and feminine energies, which we each possess as a mix in varying degrees.

Below are some common masculine and feminine energies, that have nothing to do with our physical bodies:

Common Masculine Energies	Common Feminine Energies
Righteous	Compassionate/caring
Competitive	Collaborative
Protective	Nurturing
Goal-orientated	Empathetic
Factual	Intuitive
Monotasking	Multitasking
Impatient	Patient
Assertive	Forgiving
Bias for action	Express emotions
Independent	Understand interconnectivity
Individual success	Collective success

So, if we each have a mix of these energies, how do they impact our interactions within a relationship?

Let's consider dancing for a moment. There are many different forms of dance across the world, in different cultures, and they all arise from the love of expressing physical movement with some form of music or songs – the physical merging with the non-physical.

The form of dance that is most familiar to me is ballroom dancing. I learned this style of dance over a period of about six years. I loved it!

And there are different forms of dance within the world of ballroom dancing, which all have their own unique steps, feel and alignment with different types of music.

The waltz has a beautiful and romantic feel to it, with both partners engaged in a close and flowing experience. The waltz is my favourite. The tango is intense and has more of a feel of two partners engaged in the early stages of courtship. The jive is full of energy and fun. To jive both partners need to be free and relaxed. The rumba is pure intimacy expressed on a dance floor.

Like romantic love, ballroom dancing has many different faces and vibes. Sometimes fun, sometimes romantic, sometimes intimate – but always beautiful when it's done well and executed with finesse. To dance effectively, both partners have different but reciprocal roles to play. In the waltz and tango, for example, while one partner acts as the foundation or pivot point, usually the person who aligns more with masculine energies, and the other flows around them, typically the one who aligns more with feminine energies. But always both must be in sync to make it work and flow with gracefulness.

Even when the steps aren't precisely choreographed by a dance instructor, and one partner leads and the other follows, it may be the leader who sets the direction, but unless the follower accepts the choice of steps offered the routine won't flow.

Working together, both parties can bring forth a wonderful display when they dance out of a desire for fun and pleasure. When they dance from their hearts, and not their egoic need to impress, the beauty of the dance is elevated.

Putting aside the fear of non-performance, and just embracing the opportunity to take on the performance with the purity of love, for the dance itself, lays the foundations for a wonderful outcome. On the dance floor both partners are lost in the moment, mesmerised by the opportunity for self-expression and fully present in the dance in which they are engaged. They are not thinking about future dances, or the dances that were. They are at peace with their performance, no matter what unfolds, choosing to be lost in each other's embrace. The judgements of the audience are not important to them, for they know that they are not perfect, they are just doing their best to make the experience as elegant and enjoyable as possible.

The physicality and the intimacy of dancing are special, and the eye contact they make just adds to the soul energy that the dance is executed within.

Learning how to do this well is a labour of love. There may be lessons and missteps along the way, but hard work and commitment can result in a great experience and a beautiful outcome.

Imagine if all relationships involved this much pleasure, love and trust?

Both realms could come together as one in a conscious performance with love being the inspiration for every 3D experience. We could let love lead us forward and, as we do so in complete surrender, trust in its wisdom and creative intelligence, for it knows the steps we are all inspired to take, together or alone.

Independence, Not Co-Dependence

When wonderful dance couples move around the floor they are in sync, but both dancers are always moving together by choice. There is no clinging to each other or control being applied. They complement and mirror each other in a beautiful way.

Many relationships can end up in a place of co-dependency where both parties become so intertwined with each other that they start to do everything together and forget that they are independent people having their own lives. Much of their self-esteem is sourced from their relationship and not their own hearts.

I had this experience in my early relationships, and in the long run it did not help me grow as a person.

Co-dependence can feel completely wonderful in a blossoming new relationship, when we think that we have found our perfect match, and therefore bliss will come from being together as much as possible.

However, this can become claustrophobic for both partners in time, if they are not free to sufficiently express their pure individuality on enough occasions.

No matter how compatible and in love you are with a partner, you are not the one person. Even twin flames are not the same person. They share the same soul consciousness, but not the same bodies and minds.

Regardless of who you are with, you most likely grew up in different families, enjoyed different activities, went to different schools, and so on. You can never be identical. Even so-called identical twins go through different experiences.

And besides, we are here to live our individual lives. Even partnered dancers have slightly different moves and twirls. Their steps are never the same. They just come together at crucial times to help each other through the steps. Some steps are even performed alone.

Loving yourself is as important as loving another person. Designing a relationship that respects this reality is something that a healthy presence of self-love can help both partners do.

Every couple can create the relationship that suits them. There may be stereotypes in society about what a relationship is meant to look like, but designing the relationship that allows you both to flow, individually and together, can bring you both much happiness.

I have observed a recent loosening of views about what a

relationship is meant to look like in my culture. Conditioned thinking is diminishing.

But you don't need to wait for others to change. You and your partner can design the relationship you both love, from a blank canvas.

It's never too late to start.

Polarity is Balance

Polarity is a natural phenomenon that can arise in romantic relationships, wherein masculine and feminine energies are magnetised to each other, bringing two people into balance. It is often referred to as 'opposites attract'.

The Earth itself has its own North and South Poles, and they are connected through the forces of magnetic energies. So polarity is something that we live with scientifically every day.

Although we each possess a mix of masculine and feminine energies, and they vary by person to person, masculine energies are often more dominant in men and they include energies that are more focussed on giving, doing and achieving, and feminine energies are typically more prominent in women and relate to attributes like caring, nurturing, feeling and receiving.

My book, *Where Your Happiness Hides*, gives greater detail on this topic, but the more feminine energies that a person has, the more they are likely to be magnetised to a person who is more masculine in their energies, and vice versa. When a very feminine person is attracted to a very masculine person, they are drawn to their assertive or perceived male energies. When a very masculine person is attracted to a very feminine person, they are drawn to their caring and more emotionally aware side.

This is natural balance being expressed. In the absence of balance and sufficient feminine energies, a very masculine person might be prone to inflict harm on others, and ultimately themselves. Being too out of balance one way or the other in your energies can create many other negative outcomes in our world, for individuals and collectives.

People with excessive masculine energies tend to be obsessed with winning and this can lead to separation in relationships. It may also make them less expressive and limit their ability to build emotional closeness and conscious relationships with others. They need to be balanced by a more natural infusion of the energies of love and harmony. Feminine energy by nature does not seek power over another. It seeks collaboration and unification. It is softer.

A person can also become more balanced within themselves by doing deep inner work and growing their self-awareness. They would then be less likely to be drawn to a person at an energy extreme, and vice versa. This is because their own energies become more balanced, leading them to a different set of attractions in a partner.

A highly conscious person is likely to have their energies in a more balanced state. They may have been brought up to be like this, or they may have arrived at this balance through conscious intent.

Please note that polarity, as I am describing it, is a force of attraction. It is not a force that directly influences love. Love has its own agenda and intelligence. It does what it wants.

The poles upon the Earth are known to shift. They are not fixed as many may believe. Sexual and relationship polarity are the same.

Thus, you may be magnetised to a person's mix of masculine or feminine energies, and lust may be involved also, but this does not mean that love is, or ever will be, present.

Understanding polarity can assist you to make a more informed choice of the right partner for you.

Many relationships may commence with the masculine and feminine energies of both partners complimenting and offsetting each other, but if this balance becomes distorted in some way, the level of attraction may be disturbed, putting pressure on the relationship.

Let's say that a person with very masculine energies is extremely assertive and dominant when a relationship starts out. If they release more of their masculine-based ego as time goes on, and let in more of their feminine attributes through self-awareness work, they may become less attractive to their partner – unless they are also moving into a more advanced balance of energies.

Polarity is a significant factor in all romantic relationships. Being ignorant of its influence, and alignment with mental constructs, is a key risk to any relationship held together through the primary forces of attraction.

Reflect, then select, is my advice.

Ranking Mania

We live in a world where we have learned to rank ourselves against others. This is a constant process, which I encourage you to witness within yourself. Judgement is rife, and ever-present.

When we meet or see new people, we are prone to rank them on key attributes, such as their looks, age, wealth, intellectual capabilities, ethnicity, and so on. When we meet someone of the opposite sex, this comparison is often a subconscious process we embark upon instantly, particularly if we are single and looking for a partner. And first base is usually their looks. Physicality is often the trigger for a romance commencing.

Our hearts are not doing this, our minds are, so don't be mistaken into thinking that love is presiding over this process. Our egos are, with its polarity taking shape within us.

However, nature does use sexual attraction to bring people together. What we need to consider is whether this attraction provides a strong enough bond for a relationship to unfold, or perhaps just a brief and intimate experience.

All is a choice, and the higher your awareness, the more aligned your decisions are likely to be with your best interests.

Love's Mysterious Magnetism

Just as attraction has its own on and off switch, love has its own magnetic and invisible force that can mesmerise and intoxicate us all.

When we come into the presence of different people, love, through our souls, knows which ones we have a high frequency match with, and perhaps a destiny to share part of our lives with. It can magnetise us to another soul for a purpose. And there's always a purpose. It could be for love, learning, or both.

Our polarity could be a barrier to this expression of love, or part of the spark that lights the flames and brings forth love's plan in its fullness.

We can, to some extent, alter our level of attraction to another with the actions we take. But love can also overwhelm or even inspire shifts in attraction, for it is all-knowing and powerful. It is the spirit within us and is guided by universal intelligence.

Imagine suddenly being inspired to get fit or take up a new hobby that you now love. Then, because of this change, you meet the love of your life. Do you think this is just good luck?

No, love has spoken, and the master plan is being expressed. Inspiration, after all, comes from your heart.

If love seeks a particular outcome in your life, you will feel its intent, for it never gives in. You can resist the force of love temporarily, but you will certainly suffer the consequences, manifesting as a form of stress or with physical symptoms. Your peace will be disrupted.

Imagine letting someone you felt deep love for walk away from you, because of some perceived minor imperfection, or because you had attraction to another. Love may never let you forget this mistake!

Also, the stronger your sense of self-love becomes, the higher your vibration of love will go. More people are likely to be attracted to your brighter light and new self-esteem levels. You will truly become a magnet for others, on an attraction level. You may not feel a desire to be with those others, of course, for you are subconsciously wanting a profound frequency match, but the attraction will still be there.

I hope you see that love and attraction can be a complex cocktail of forces, but a cocktail which only has one recipe option – always follow your heart, because it is your way through to the experiences that love is guiding you towards.

To resist is to resist your destiny!

Are We Blinded by Beauty?

If you have ever sat and watched a sunset or a sunrise on a beach, you will marvel at its natural beauty. However, you consciously understand that you can never own a sunset or sunrise. They belong to Mother Nature.

Unfortunately, we take the opposite approach to human beauty, often hoping to enter into a relationship with lovers who are beautiful or handsome.

But we must be careful not to let ourselves become blinded by the beauty of others, for it is only skin-deep, and in any event differs from person to person – beauty is in the eye of the beholder.

When we approach beauty in a low frequency way and try to essentially own it for our own egoic benefit, we move away from the opportunity to connect with the person beneath their beauty.

What our eyes see is often more of the physicality of a person, rather than the light and love within them. We are less likely to open to these aspects of another, because they must be primarily felt and not thought. But we must go beyond our conditioned mindsets and change the way that we value others.

First, we have to explore whether beauty has distorted the ego of a person who has been born with natural beauty. I'm sure we've all seen examples of vanity, and even arrogance, on show. Such people have much yet to learn through their life's experiences and conditioning. If they have been taught that their beauty essentially makes them superior to others or have been treated like a prince or princess by the world they inhabit, because they are very good looking, they can become arrogant and expectant of privilege, which may cause them to focus on superficial aspects of relationships and limit their chance of finding a high love match.

This is not normally their fault. Their egos have simply become inflated by the way they have been treated by others and what they have been taught. They may focus on attraction and not love. We all become conditioned in different ways and carry different wounds.

The next step is to become aware of exactly why you may be attracted to the person. In any romantic relationship, physical appearance plays a major role in attraction. However, the expression of love is different to love itself. What other qualities do they have? Love is not found in the body; it is found in the heart and sparked through eye contact.

Love is always first base for me now in romance, regardless of looks. To a degree, I often felt intimidated around very good-looking people when I was younger, feeling unworthy of their presence. But I have greater self-worth now. Like everyone, I still know how wonderful it is to be in love with a lady who I believe is beautiful. But now I look beyond the surface and seek deeper connections.

Looks can also change as we age. So basing any relationship too heavily on lust for another's good looks can lead to that relationship inevitably ending over time.

Also, if lust is not accompanied by strong emotional connection, problems can arise once the so-called honeymoon period expires.

Our perception of our physical looks is also a major source of our own self-esteem. However, because we are collectively brought up to need to be seen as perfect, even the most beautiful amongst us are critical of their own looks to some extent. We are always our own harshest critics.

Many relationships might also fail when adequate sexual attraction is not present at all, even if love is present in a healthy dose. However, ideally this choice is made consciously, and not subconsciously.

These days when I go out socially, I use my heart as the detector of love above all else to draw me towards a prospective partner. Of course, real love connections are rare, so my detector rarely goes off.

If we want deep love to be present in our romantic relationships, patience is key. Your heart knows when you are ready for the next dose of romantic love and does not care about the time on your watch, or the date in your diary.

There is one other metaphysical nuance to our looks that is worthy of note. The truth is that before birth we chose the body we currently live within. Our parents just provided the DNA to manifest it into reality. Our bodies are thus designed to attract to us the significant partners with whom we were meant to intersect. Our physicality is important in this regard, and almost certainly our lovers will be authentically drawn to our looks, or some other prominent aspect of us.

This can cause a challenge for good-looking people, because a higher number of people of the opposite sexual energy will be drawn to their physicality. The trick for them is to be selective.

When we lament the looks that we have, we are naïvely forgetting this truth and moving into illusion. You are who and what you are for a purpose, and you are always where you are meant to be. Accepting that is especially important to releasing any hang-ups you may have about your looks. Our light is perfect and at our core we are pure love, even if we may not think that our looks are enough.

Perfection is Overrated

It is important to recognise that love does not need to operate within a perfect relationship. It does not seek perfection, merely your advancement and happiness, and it has a way of arranging relationships for you with the right, wrong person who will draw out the issues that need to be dealt with, by you. What comes up is always raised for you and through you. It is not meant to harm you but to help you at a soul level.

Still, we tend to believe that if our relationships are not continually wonderful, we are with the wrong person and should change our partner.

But even if we exit the relationship, it is likely that you will not be given a 'saloon passage' to an easier and more harmonious relationship, unless you do the work to learn from the last one. Without this work, love will again match you with another person like the last one, who will draw out the preconditioned shadows and wounds in your mind. The soul does not give up – ever!

Like you, your partner is perfect in their imperfection. Value that and you will grow more swiftly together.

CHAPTER 9

What Happens When the Music Stops?

Let the Blame Games Begin

Very few people enter a relationship with the expectation that they will end. You don't get married to get divorced. Our egos normally create expectations that this latest partner is 'the one that I will be with until I die'. We are normally caught up in the euphoria of the new relationship and have high hopes for the future.

But hopes are just constructs of the egoic mind that may or not come true. Our souls ignore the controlling and limiting energy present in hope.

And what we hope for is far less than what love wants to bestow upon us. Remember, unlike your mind, love does not prescribe to the concept of limits.

Like all dances, every relationship has a physical ending in our third dimensional world. Either the relationship ends when one of the partners dies, or the relationship ends because one or both lovers have chosen to end it. Each scenario is normally the source of much pain.

This is not the case, however, in the eternal world of the metaphysical, for there energies apply, not forms. There, love never dies, so the frequency of soul connections can and often do continue into eternity.

So what do we do when the music often stops for one partner

unexpectantly, and their partner exits the dance floor before all the steps (they expected to take) have been completed?

Most readers have possibly experienced a relationship breakup and know how hard it can be, no matter whether you are the one leaving or the one being left. But the key is appreciation for what has been, and for what might yet come.

Like many people I have been through both sides of this event multiple times. From my experience they can get easier, but only if you do the work to learn more about yourself from each breakup situation.

All my romantic relationships taught me much, once I took the time to look back at them with curiosity. And each one taught me something new and unique about myself.

But the important thing they all taught me was that I needed to be truer to myself, if I were to make a relationship successful. If I wasn't authentic, and in my truth, who was in the relationship? Not the real me!

No matter how aware you are, when a relationship you wanted to continue ends you can feel great emotional despair. Betrayal and abandonment are the common, major energies experienced by the person being dismissed, even if they have contributed significantly to the breakup.

The blame game can also begin in earnest.

But any emotional pain you experience is always mental. It does not emanate from the soul. The sensation of a broken heart is caused by pain generated by the mind's sense of loss. Not the heart's.

People speak of hearts being broken in a breakup. This is not the case as the soul does not feel pain and does not break. It is a source of pure love and compassion and will never judge another soul. Souls also know the intent of karmic and soul contracts, so they are aware of what is unfolding before it unfolds. They bring forth the breakup for you and through you in agreement with another soul for purpose.

What gets damaged in a breakup are the egos of the parties involved. A myriad of emotions arrive, aligning primarily with a sense of failure and a diminution of one's self-worth. But this is where the opportunity for higher self-awareness arises, and understanding the deeper intent behind the lessons being orchestrated for your benefit can help to limit the damage and allow you to grow to even higher levels of evolution.

The good news is that we can all learn to be more self-aware in this way, and it will only serve to take us to new levels of happiness and self-forgiveness, then into new relationships where love can flourish with the energies of truth, trust and acceptance all present.

And guess what happens when you reach new heights of happiness and self-love?

You become more attractive to the sexual preferences of the people you desire!

Finding Peace in Rejection

Being rejected by someone you love, or someone you may have generated many memories with, can be a debilitating experience.

Rejection is one of the hardest energies to find peace within, for your mind normally concludes that you were not enough or not worthy of the other person who left you.

I've faced rejection from women I cared about, which was tough and brought up old beliefs that I wasn't enough. Overcoming separation was challenging, but my deepest pain came from self-rejection.

Acceptance is the key to finding the peace that you crave in a rejection situation. Unfortunately, acceptance can be extremely hard to establish when your ego has been dented, or you felt a soul connection with the person who decided to separate from you.

The key to recovery and coping lies in the relationship between your self-love and the love you feel for the other person.

It's important in a separation situation that you prioritise yourself, and your own self-love, over your love for your partner or the person to whom you were attracted. You matter to you. It's your life and your pain that needs to be faced. You can't feel or face the pain of another. That's their job, not yours.

Of course, expressing compassion to the other person is important in the situation too. Unless their heart is closed to yours, in which case it is in your best interests to walk away and honour your own love. There will inevitably be pain, but this pain is just a message of love from your heart.

Learning to honour and face pain is an essential part of overcoming traumas and moving to higher conscious awareness.

I suffered greatly from certain romantic relationship breakdowns because I was too stubborn and self-deprecating for my own good. When people who I loved walked away from me, I was all too ready to take the blame for what had taken place and try to change myself as a matter of priority.

This helped me to grow in some ways, but in hindsight, I would have been better off letting go much faster and accepting that my partner was entitled to make the choice that they had reached.

All in life is a choice, and we all get to make them in every moment that we experience. Understanding and honouring this truth would have been good for my psyche and helped me to get over the pain much faster.

When any relationship ends it is important to understand that you have not failed. It was the relationship that was built on shaky foundations, because there were hidden wounds in both people. However, with the benefit of the magic mirror there will always be things we can learn about ourselves in such situations.

This is true for both parties. The stronger a person's ego, the less likely they might be to take responsibility for their role in the relationship turmoil. If their heart is not open in these types of experiences, their mind will seek to protect their reputation as a priority.

But if both hearts are open, the energy of compassion can enter the situation at hand and a compromise may be possible. If love brought forth the relationship in the first place, that same love could solve the situation for the benefit of both parties.

Regardless, if we can learn anything from an ended relationship, then it will always constitute success.

Taming the Masculine Response to Rejection

We all feel the pain of rejection when it arises within us. This is a function of being human. Pain is a natural part of our make-up.

When relationships suffer from separation and perhaps end, a great scourge in our society often arises through the actions of masculine energies, predominantly men, who are not capable of managing the pain they endure. Instead, this pain too often becomes a catalyst for revenge against the person who rejected them, too often resulting in that person being harmed, abused or even killed. This is all too common and can instil great fear into women in particular about the wisdom of even entering a romantic relationship.

Any translation of pain into mental or physical abuse usually results from a person's inability to own and process their own pain, so it ends up owning them. This can cause it to overflow and manifest into abuse. They lack the self-awareness to know that pain is essentially a message of love asking them to go inward and heal wounds that are ready to be overcome. Their violence is an indication that they are intrinsically unhappy and lack self-worth. Happy and self-aware people in the energy of love do not start fights involving physical violence, nor seek power over another individual.

Such people need to understand that the universe never gives us painful experiences unless it knows we are ready to face them and transcend them. Relationship issues are a prime source of new levels of self-awareness, but this relies on an individual finding the inner strength to approach it in this way.

Men need to be empowered with the wisdom to go within, own their own feelings and react from a place of love. Society's subliminal message to men that having power over others makes them more valuable and stronger, needs to be replaced with wiser messages.

The stereotyping of men has meant many men do not have the capacity to access their feelings or to deal with them in a conscious and harmless way. Like a so-called warrior, their emotions often convert into violence. This is a conditioned and ignorant response to the opportunity they have been given to grow.

Governments face the problem of reacting to this epidemic of violence and abuse. Traditionally they have turned to the creation of laws and the provision of community services to respond to the aftermath of these types of incidents. But how many innocent women need to suffer before this issue is properly addressed?

Police and social workers are not likely to be present when a man loses his temper and becomes abusive. Their ability to prevent unfortunate outcomes is therefore limited.

Prevention of domestic violence must start in the world of education, not legislation. Men need to be encouraged, and taught at an early age, how to connect to their pain, and to effectively turn it into self-awareness and peace, not violence.

This would be best undertaken in schools before boys and young men begin their foray into the dating world, although educating offenders also has great merit.

We must create a new generation of men who are conscious of themselves and understand the gift within their feelings.

The word 'gentleman' can become a reality when we teach men how they can properly respond to relationship traumas and forever drop the stereotype we have adopted that a warrior is superior to a gentleman.

The Fallacy of Jealousy

Rejection often brings forth great jealousy when you are replaced by another person, by your former partner.

It is considered normal to dislike, and even despise, the person who becomes the new partner of your ex-lover, particularly if your former partner left you for that third party. This is a defence system erected by the human ego.

I had this experience on three occasions, so I know how much it hurts – when you are not in soul-energy.

When you are in a higher vibration of love, you find it far easier to accept these kinds of situations. Your human personality will struggle with pain, but this pain is a message of love and is most likely encouraging you to let go. Your heart knows that your ex-lover has the right to choose who they are with and knows that it must honour this choice. It accepts what is with grace, and helps the pain of separation to be processed in the fire of self-love.

Do you really want to be with someone who puts another above you?

That is a question your self-love needs to answer!

In love's wisdom we can also find peace in knowing that all happens for a reason. Both you and your ex-lover have agreed to separate at a soul level for some purpose. It is a destiny of sorts. Love wants us to learn from the experience and to move on to something more suited to our lives. Perhaps, the loving match between both lovers has been disturbed in some way, and change is needed?

As hard as this can be on your mind to process, when we are able to witness the events in truth and love, we can surrender to the wisdom in the shift.

Often the good things that will arise from the separation will not become clear until sometime in the future.

Acceptance is the gateway to peace when jealousy rears its ugly, but normal head.

The Lost Power of Conflict Management

When we enter relationships, we often hope for a myriad of positive experiences, including fun, intimacy, and shared happiness. But, as this book points out, all relationships are also an experiment with the universal intention of bringing us closer to our true level of self-love. This is brought forward by the combined energies of love and fear.

You might say that their intention is to create tension and therefore bring attention to inner illusions, so that you can transcend them.

I entered two marriages and multiple relationships earlier in my life with high hopes for a blissful union. Unfortunately, I discovered that this was a long shot, given my level of consciousness and the plans love had for me.

I did not understand the mirroring aspect of relationships and was naïvely ill-equipped to handle conflict in the relationships, as were most of my partners.

I was not taught in my formative years to understand that it's not just the good times that matter in a relationship, anyone can do those, but how you handle the disputes and 'bad' times that truly matters.

If the mirroring of our wounds through disputes is not addressed consciously, they can fester, allow resentments to build up and eventually destroy the relationship.

This requires us to consciously connect to our feelings, express them with truth and listen with compassion to the expressions of truth by our partner.

A couple who grows together consciously can experience a loving relationship that becomes closer and stronger over time for they are effectively learning to harness the power of love and letting it redefine what is possible for them both.

Perhaps this is another opportunity in our society. Rather than teaching young people in schools how to do mathematics and science so they can make money, shouldn't we also teach them how to consciously love?

After all the cost of relationship separations and divorces carries a significant emotional and financial cost that could be mitigated with higher self-awareness.

Boundaries and Barriers

Our world can sometimes feel excessively competitive and lonely for many people. Mental health issues are on the rise as we collectively struggle with the pressures of life.

Our egoic distortions that tell us that achieving success and avoiding failure are our 'tickets' to being loved, manifest into an excessively difficult and competitive world. Harmony is the victim of our own egos.

A big part of living in the energy of love is feeling valued and cared for by our relationships. However, with so many people not having the skills or self-awareness to deal with their insecurities and personal frailties, is it any wonder that they are not emotionally capable of valuing the feelings of others?

If you are spending much of your energy on trying to find your own balance and happiness within your own pain, it is extremely difficult for you to care for the wellbeing of others.

We thus have a crisis of consciousness in society and, although many are awakening to the opportunity that they can grow their conscious awareness and find their own self-love, most people are trying to survive in a competitive and unyielding world where self-interest and low self-awareness has become the order of the day. And this is leaving many people feeling broken and unhappy. They have lost trust in love, despite it being the core of what they are.

The world has established systems and structures based on our conditioned ways of thinking. Some revel within these systems and structures, and others fall behind or even give up. The world can be harsh for some and beautiful for others. Higher consciousness across the populations is a good starting point to address this lop-sided world.

We have an intrinsic need to connect to other souls, for we are born into families, tribes and communities. Connection is our natural state. However, we often find ourselves becoming the victim of wounded people who are conditioned to put their own interests over others in an unfair way.

This can cause them to act out of a lower state of consciousness, putting money or their own status ahead of love, and harming another unnecessarily.

When we experience unloving behaviour from others, we often have a choice between our self-love, and the love we have for others.

Self-love demands that sometimes it may be in our interests to establish boundaries with people who do us harm. We don't have to hate them or seek revenge, for that can spark an unnecessary war and isn't in alignment with love, but we may need to put ourselves first and protect our own interests from people who don't care about our feelings.

When we seek revenge, we are dropping our vibration down to lower levels, and it denies the reality that you were part of the original problem. The universe will dishonour us (through the actions of others) if we dishonour ourselves. Remember, we get what we need before we get what we want.

'Turn the other cheek,' as is often said. There is, however, a difference between putting up boundaries and creating barriers with others with whom we connect.

Often when we are let down, we can lose trust in other people and withdraw from aspects of our lives to find safety. In this dark place we can put up barriers to all and sundry. However, this can hinder our opportunities to express ourselves fully in life.

I went through a period where I shied away from romance for fear of being hurt again. This reaction was subconscious at first.

However, I knew I needed to go inward to discover how I had contributed to these circumstances, and to grow my self-awareness around romance.

I put a barrier around myself so that I did not suffer again. This barrier was created by my egoic fears.

Barriers can be harmful to your freedoms in life if they are in place unnecessarily or for too long.

Boundaries, however, can be a necessary evil, even if they cause you to feel guilt, because separating yourself from a person who is uncaring towards you, can be your best option at times to preserve your happiness. By doing this you may well be finally honouring yourself.

Your feelings are yours to own and no one else can tell you how to feel. You will need to feel into any decision in this regard and trust you inner knowing, for it is based on the energy of love and will whisper or scream its advice into your mind.

When a romantic relationship ends, boundaries can be an understandable option to help you find peace. But barriers are next level and can be unhealthy to your recovery.

Forgiveness is Only Ever for You

Love knows the power of forgiveness. When we understand that all happens for us and through us, not to us in life, at the behest of love, we will find it more natural to forgive others who let us down.

It is quite normal in society for people to hang onto grudges when they believe others have treated them unfairly or let them down. This is quite common in romantic situations where separation has taken place, either permanently or temporarily.

In many cases, our egos create a story about the separation or perceived unfairness and continue to use that story to justify and amplify the pain that we are clinging to, rather than facing the pain and letting it go.

When we allow the pain of the past to continue, we are effectively stabbing ourselves in the heart repeatedly.

In many cases the other party did what they did in their own interests and do not care how you feel about the situation. They may have moved on already. Further, they cannot feel what you are feeling for your feelings are yours to own and learn from.

Love can be ruthless like this, but great wisdom lies within your pain should you seek to listen and learn from its messages of love.

Forgiveness is only ever for the person who feels harmed and is in pain. If a 'wronged person' does not forgive the other person involved, their own pain will continue to harm them for the rest of their life, even if the situation does not flare up again.

Pain created by our conscious or subconscious minds is not released until we witness it and make a conscious effort to let it go. It will often linger inside us, causing damage to our psyche and our bodies by virtue of anxiety and stress, even if we are not conscious of it.

When unwanted events take place in our lives, we can go one step higher than forgiveness and move into the energy of gratitude. This is an extremely advanced place to arrive at, but is unlikely until a person learns to consciously process their pain as a matter of course, and value the increasing consciousness and self-love that arises from the ashes of a problem.

I wrote to my second wife after our painful separation and thanked her for leaving me, for I realised that her leaving me had given me the impetus to grow in ways I had never witnessed before.

The pain of this event had taken me through forgiveness and then into gratitude. This took me a few years of intense inner work to arrive at this liberating place.

Being able to offer another person forgiveness may seem like a loving offering, but truly you are offering it to yourself out of self-love.

When Jesus was crucified, he reportedly asked God to forgive all who had trespassed against him, for they knew not what they did. He was able to do this because he knew that they were fulfilling his divine path to crucifixion and were conditioned to act as they did. He was in the total energy of pure love.

Now, this is an extreme path to separation, and none of us are likely to experience this level of torment. However, when we learn to forgive those who have let us down, take our lessons and move on, we can overcome energetic entanglements far easier and move back into a state of peace.

The Truths About Abandonment and Betrayal

When an important relationship in our lives ends or stumbles, we are prone to feel abandoned and/or betrayed.

Once you move to a higher sense of conscious awareness, you see such powerful negative emotions for what they truly are: just illusions of the ego, which need to be cleared. Most of us need to do a lot of inner work to arrive in this elevated place of wisdom, but we can with enough self-love.

Abandonment and betrayal are obstacles to this, because they are linked to our inner belief that we are unworthy of love and must suffer as a result. At its absolute extension, we all collectively think that we have been born into a world that does not care for us. There is a part of us that feels let down by God, for bad things keep happening to us, and even though we pray to him, we still suffer. This can be a confusing message.

These deep feelings are further exaggerated if the people we love most let us down. Perhaps this is our parents, siblings, employers, or a partner we loved deeply. If these people could not even love me, despite all that I gave them, who else could we ask ourselves?

Our core wounding, associated with our belief in separation, leads us in into these highly emotive feelings, further exaggerating our belief that life is unsafe, dangerous, and sometimes brutal.

And let's not forget that, for centuries, life on Earth has been like this for the unprivileged masses. Wars, plagues, natural disasters, and financial pressures have made our Earthly experiences hard and testing for many souls. The memories of these painful experiences have been handed down from generation to generation as stories of hardship, fuelling our fears that while on this planet we deserve to suffer, and so we inevitably will. We essentially co-suffer with others.

As we have felt cut off from our own hearts, generation after generation, our love for life has been diminished and our vibrations have been dimmed by negative thoughts and beliefs. So, we seek to protect ourselves.

Collectively, we still seek to survive not thrive, to hide from bad possibilities and to play it safe. Our underlying belief that we will be let down by life is manifested into reality by our own negative frequencies and fears. It is a self-fulfilling prophecy on a grand scale.

The process of removing these negative frequencies is our path to higher conscious awareness and every time we confront one, we lift ourselves closer to enlightenment.

We can live our lives from our own light or from the fears that cast a shadow across them. The choice is ours.

We are rarely betrayed or abandoned; we betray and abandon ourselves.

We get what we put out, always!

Understanding Relating Styles

The psychology profession has done great work on what they call attachment styles. John Bowlby and Mary Ainsworth are famous for developing these theories.

These styles, typically learned in your childhood from your early experiences, can determine how you interact with other people. They are, however, exaggerated in relationships where strong love is present.

I thank these two psychologists for the work they did, because it helped me to deconstruct some major issues in my love life, and to see myself more clearly.

The more intense the love you are experiencing, the more intense the triggers that seem to be pulled through these attachment styles.

There are four core attachment styles that people normally fit into, although it normally acts as a continuum and you could be a blending of the styles.

The core categories are: anxious, secure, avoidant, or disorganised.

The experiences we encounter in life will determine how much we typically trust love. For example, people who have been exposed to reliable love will tend to be secure in loving relationships. Whereas people who have had inconsistent love in their lives may have lost the belief that they are worthy of love.

People who are anxiously attached will tend to chase love, for they fear that it will abandon them.

Avoidant people tend to be overwhelmed by love and will attempt to run from it when it gets too intense for their liking, as they have learned that love will let them down. They therefore seek to have control over it.

Disorganised lovers tend to desire intimacy but their fear of getting hurt leads them to a push/pull dynamic in romantic relationships.

Anxious and dismissive lovers will often have much work to do to overcome their inherent woundings and become more secure.

I was an anxious lover for much of my life, because of the variable love that I experienced growing up. This naturally drew me towards women with more avoidant or disorganised personalities, so that I could witness my emotional wounds and remove them through higher self-awareness.

Unfortunately, I was not aware of my predilections until I looked back into the past relationship woes, and did the awareness work necessary to free myself of my attachment style. These days I am naturally more secure.

I would recommend that, if you have had relationship issues in your life, then really consider your attachment style. There is much content about this topic in books and on the internet to inform a curious reader. Understanding yourself more deeply on any front can only ever serve to assist you with your life choices, and the more beliefs that you move from your subconscious to your conscious mind, the more conscious and secure you can become overall.

Consider this process to be like an iceberg. Your conscious beliefs are like the ice above the water. You know they are there. However, your subconscious beliefs are like the ice under the water – largely oblivious to you. Out of sight, out of mind.

I had too much ice under my waters when I was younger, and so my life turned out to be a tragedy at times, like the story of the Titanic!

However, luckily, I survived and have been able to turn my pain into knowing, unlike the people in that tragic event.

Now I doubt there are many core subconscious beliefs left lurking out of sight, in my life. They have all melted back into my sea of awareness.

That's been my goal anyway!

Giving and Receiving Love in Equal Measure

Related to our attachment style and our sense of self, sits our relationship with giving and receiving love in relationships.

A balanced loving relationship is built on an equal flow of loving energies between both parties. Two people who are secure, because their level of self-love is high, will typically expect to both give and receive love in a balanced way.

These people tend to be self-centred, knowing that in a relationship they matter as much as the other person.

Many of us are taught to be self-less in life. We have been taught that it is virtuous to give to others, but to not ask for much in return. We often subconsciously believe that, because of this programming, we warrant less love than the one we love. Our role is to love and not be loved.

Anxious lovers tend to take this position because they are quite selfless.

People who are selfish are on the opposite end of the spectrum and are typically more inclined to expect to receive more love than they give in a relationship. Avoidant lovers tend to be more like this, but will over-dose on love if it gets too strong and run away.

Ultimately, everyone wants to be loved, we have just developed different coping strategies to get through life. But many of these coping strategies prevent us from being in the energy of our own self-love.

If you are out of balance as a couple in terms of the flow of energy between you, this can be seen as a chance for growth.

It represents an opportunity for higher self-awareness to be gained as both partners can work together to release their conditioned relating styles and subconscious patterns. To do otherwise could result in problems for the relationship over time.

Remember, balance is always rewarded by a universe that wants you to grow your self-love but balance it with your ability to be in loving union with others and have fun.

It is possible to learn and have fun at the same time. That's the secret to moving forward in life with wonder.

Drop the worry, relax, have fun and observe all that unfolds with awareness.

PART D

ADVANCED APPLICATIONS OF LOVE

CHAPTER 10

The Power of Conscious Relating

The Advanced Way to Love

Conscious relating is not complex, but still quite rare, for it is a skill not many of us are taught.

In different aspects of this book, I have touched on elements of this advanced way of interacting with others, and there is a helpful definition in Chapter 1. Let us now look at it in more detail.

Conscious relating, as its name suggests, involves applying higher awareness to the truths between two or more parties. The higher the consciousness of the parties involved, the more effective this form of relating becomes.

Conscious relating relies upon feeling, self-reflection and truthful expression. It requires full transparency between two individuals.

There are no limits to a relationship that is based on feelings and is not consumed by thoughts. In such a place, a relationship can continuously expand, for it is not based on the inflation of egos that typically result from a more normal exchange. It is a soul-based process that steps us away from the more rudimentary security-conscious way of being that many of us have been taught.

The roles of these two 'operating systems' in a conscious person work the way nature intended. The soul (or heart) operates from feelings, and the mind (or ego) operates from a place of logic. Feelings are expressed and both people, through their logical minds, interpret them from a place of compassion and logic.

Negative judgements are absent in the exchanges that take place, because all parties are focussed on improving the relationship by helping each other grow in awareness, and in turn growing closer together. Blame does not apply, and truth is a key focus. It is a form of continuous improvement for the individuals, and the relationship that they share. Love is the driving force behind the exchanges, not a need to be proven right. The exchange is not an egoic competition, but a loving exchange filled with care, compassion, and curiosity.

Righteousness is a key need that leads to separation between lovers, yet awareness of this can so easily remedy the cracks in our relationships.

The more conscious that an individual becomes, the more connected they are to their soul energy, and therefore their feelings. And when an individual's soul energy becomes the dominant force within an individual's being, their feelings are infused into their mind and become their dominant thought patterns.

In this way, the mind becomes more of a receiver of the messages inherent in feelings, rather than the initiator of stand-alone thoughts.

Imagine two people interacting with each other with truth-based feelings being expressed as the cornerstone of their conversations. And imagine their feelings being met with no judgement, but instead with care, compassion, and love. This form of interaction is purely constructive and positive.

Relationships based on this type of energy bring endless possibilities to both parties involved.

The symbol of infinity is synonymous with this form of relating. The diagram below shows pictorially how conscious relating works.

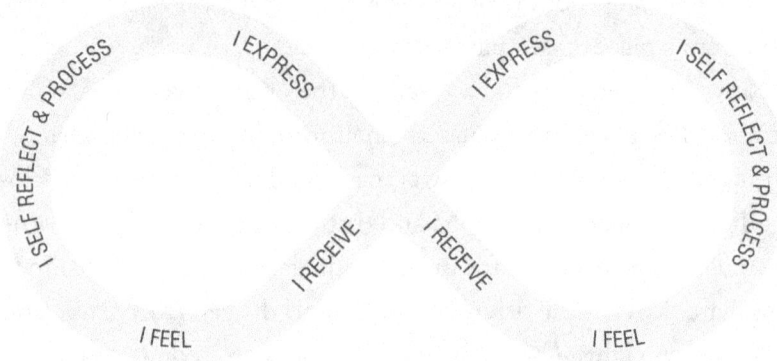

Figure 4: Communicating Through the Infinite Power of Love

The fundamental difference between more normal forms of relating and conscious relating involves the application of love.

In normal relating situations, the human ego plays a more dominant role in conversations. This introduces a more defensive aspect to conversations and can spark the blame game taking place. Ego-based thinking in an interaction tends to lead both parties to defending the stories that their minds have created.

Loving and peaceful solutions are less likely when egos are heavily involved.

The table below shows the core factors that differ under conscious-relating and ego-based relationships:

Ego-Based Relationships	Conscious-Relating Relationships
Defensive	Vulnerable
Thought-based	Feelings-based
Suppressive	Expressive
Competitive	Compassionate
Separating	Unifying
Inflationary	Expansive
Blaming	Balanced
Vindictive	Forgiving
Selfish or self-less	Self-centred

More comparisons are possible, but these examples paint a clear picture of the two extremes of behaviours and emotions that can apply to each paradigm.

The higher the consciousness of the individuals taking part in any interaction, the more conscious the overall process is likely to be. Conscious relating is best supported by individuals who are on the journey to higher self-awareness. However, a more conscious way of working together and sharing their feelings on an ongoing basis can only make for more expansive and happy relationships. Any couple can apply the practices of conscious relating and develop this skill together. Practice makes perfect.

In this process, egos don't get inflated, awareness is expanded by a commitment to love.

Why not start applying the principles today? You owe it to your relationship to do so!

The sky is the limit for relationships that effective apply these principles on a regular basis.

Going Inward Then Outward is Critical

The application of conscious relating to your romantic relationship is dependent on the ability of both parties to go inward and self-reflect on issues that arise in interactions, before they go outward and seek change.

Taking responsibility for your own role in a relationship is super-critical.

Both lovers must understand that they must be the change that they require in the relationship, and understand how their beliefs and actions – about both the present moment and their perceptions of past experiences and life circumstances – have contributed to the issues at hand. We all bring our own issues into every interaction with others, and unless we are self-aware about the power of those issues on our perception of the present, those issues will continue to impact us, usually negatively.

Relationships are partially mirrors capable of showing you deeper aspects of yourself and each other. They are not just about fun and pleasure, but about clearing away our emotional 'junk' so our lives can become more joyful together.

In normal ego-centric relationships, conflicts normally result in an element of defensive reactions from both parties as their egos project and protect their own versions of the story currently playing out.

Conscious relating is different. You need to be vulnerable, transparent and open about your truths to make it work. You need to want to grow for both your sakes and for the sake of love blossoming. Most of all, you will need to be able to value your feelings and connect with them to open your heart and develop self-love.

Pain not faced does not go away, and when the magic mirror of your partner's love exposes your limiting beliefs and past wounds, you will need to be able to accept areas where you could be more consciously advanced.

Defensiveness does not work when we are trying to expand a relationship that matters to you. Letting your walls down fully, and looking at yourself in the mirror, can be confronting for the egoic mind, for it is prone to want to be right. However, when two people in any relationship are fully vulnerable and compassionate to the other's views and feelings, trust can be fully present, and resentments can become a thing of the past.

Trust can only ever be present when we accept fully what is.

Conscious relating is not just a process you can adopt with other parties. You can apply it to your own self-love development by working on your own truths alone.

Love is Always Present

Love is always in the energy of now. Our minds so often revel in revisiting our painful past experiences and are always wanting to plan for a better future. Future, past, future, past is the calling card of our ego centric minds.

When we consciously relate to another, we will find ourselves only in the now, for our hearts know that digging up the past is only worthwhile if it brings forth learnings.

After all, how can we be fully present with ourselves, or another, if we are never where we are?

Love is a feeling and not a thought, so how can we feel love in the future or the past?

Be present and love can last.

Love is Fully Transparent

In most human interactions, we tend to say what we are comfortable disclosing to another. There is usually an element of self-protection in play.

But what if we dropped all our pretence and entered a space of total trust with our lover? What if nothing was off-limits in our conversations because you knew that the other person was totally dedicated to the relationship?

Transparency is an excellent quality of infinite communication, for there are no limits. It is truth. It might challenge you at first, but in the presence of deep love, transparency is so potent.

Vulnerability between two minds brings you into sync with the love in your hearts. And that is a divine place to be.

Never Struggle to Communicate Again

Have you ever been witness to a couple in a restaurant who eat their food in silence, because they are seemingly unable to come up with topics to discuss. Conscious relating is the antidote to this awkward silence.

Many people struggle to access and express their true feelings. This means that in conversations with each other they normally discuss the issues that surround them, not the insights arising from within them. They might discuss their children, their house, their jobs, or even things going on in the news. However, these things may become fully known to them both, making conversation boring and repetitive.

Conscious relating is different because it is reliant on the wisdom in, and the expression of, our feelings. We are all living, feeling beings and we truly never stop feeling, unless we die. When you get used to connecting to your deepest feelings and inner realisations, you will never run out of topics to discuss!

We are ever-expanding beings, whether we like it or not. When you become aware of this expansion and work with it, you will never struggle for topics to discuss together. And that will make for a far more enjoyable night in that favourite restaurant of yours.

I had a conscious relationship with a woman who, like me, was in touch with her feelings. Our conversations would sometimes last for many hours without any breaks. It was an incredible experience.

Being able to express your feelings with another person with no limits and know that they will be deeply honoured, is a wonderful gift and will set your heart free.

Don't stay in your self-generated cage of conditioning. Love has the key to free you, if you let it speak through you.

Designing the Relationship That You Want

Normal relationships are more likely to follow traditional patterns of behaviour than conscious ones, because the adopted beliefs of the people involved are less subject to open discussion and challenge.

The absence of a full expression of feelings and truths can also lead to assumptions being made by the respective partners, and deep desires and concerns not being aired.

I have experienced these kinds of relationships too, where expression was stilted and emotions were avoided. This led to perceived problems being solved and not real ones, and silence making it hard sometimes to find the best way forward.

When you are fully vulnerable and transparent about your feelings, you can better address your needs and wants in a relationship.

This can revolutionise a relationship by allowing both parties to consciously design the relationship that they both want, rather than making assumptions about what the relationship should look and feel like.

A conscious relationship has infinite possibilities to expand and grow, rather than have it atrophy, as so many relationships do.

Worship is No More

Conscious relating cannot operate fully in a relationship that is not balanced. But it will inspire greater harmony and equality as it is embraced.

If one party has power over the other and controls the relationship because of a higher sense of self-worth, or a bigger ego, equality is diminished. This kind of worship in a relationship blocks the flow of love and can prevent the equal flow and appreciation of feelings between both parties.

I have been witness to, and been a part of, certain lop-sided relationships in my life. I helped create these unknowingly, but I will never tolerate it again in my life．I rather be alone.

At a basic level, many relationships, particularly marriages, seem to adopt the 'keep-them-happy' syndrome as a core element of their dynamics. But this can disempower a person from fully expressing their feelings with their partner, and it's time we saw this for what it is – a version of love based on the fear of abandonment.

But when a couple apply conscious relating to their relationship repertoire, it can help to build a stronger basis of equality and connectivity, and love can create a beautiful new relationship with limitless possibilities.

Intimacy Comes Alive

It is often said that in long term relationships the sexual attraction and activity often diminishes over time.

There are different strategies that a couple can employ to reverse this trend, but conscious relating is a wonderful antidote for this loss of passion, because emotional closeness is critical in any relationship – without strong connectivity, lovemaking tends to become just physical sex.

An equal flow of energies is vital to the full enjoyment of intimacy. You will feel such imbalances in your heart, body and mind when they exist. And a lack of energetic polarity translates into less passionate lovemaking.

This makes sense because sexual intimacy is a profound way of expressing love. It drives great passion. When we don't have that in a sexual experience, it can feel like there is a core ingredient or energy missing. It can still be great, but perhaps not as great as it could be with a deep and expanding love being present between both individuals.

Conscious relating validates the feelings of both parties and allows for beautiful compromises, which can bring forth greater trust, acceptance and truth between those involved. With enhanced emotional connection and the ongoing elimination of resentments and stresses between both parties, closeness can be stimulated.

This may even develop into tantric lovemaking, which is possible with two conscious partners in sync with their sexual energies.

Sexual intimacy with another human being with whom we are attracted is a wonderful experience, and one of the greatest joys of being alive on Earth. The human climax in a sexual experience is generally a great feeling, though through conscious relating its deeper significance can also be better understood.

The truth is that this experience is the closest approximation that we can feel to being in the total bliss of being fully connected to God, or universal intelligence. When two people who are in the energy of true love engage sexually, this can take both individuals into a higher state of conscious awareness instantly. It is a potent form of vibrational elevation, for love is completely present, and in its infinite creative power.

Sharing the Right Currency of Love

Love is the true currency in relationships, even the one with yourself. It is the creator that we sometimes lose touch with as our relationships shift and change. But when it is allowed to flourish between two lovers and create with its magic, it provides a powerful magnetic current between and around you both. It is radiant and never ceases to flow with and as passion.

Many relationships commence in the pure energy of love, but with time can become influenced by life's other obligations and stresses. We may have children to care for, properties to manage, families to fit into, and money may become a dominant focus of our energies. We get busy and distracted and lose the focus on our relationships.

This shift certainly occurred in one of my marriages. With five children, high pressure jobs, financial pressures and significant

mortgages, the relationship was distracted away from the purity of what created it in the first place: love.

There were times when I admit I got too focussed on providing money to my wife and children rather than love.

You can imagine what happened to the love between us, as husband and wife?

However, when a relationship has a conscious connection and feeling-based relating style as its backbone, love can remain as the dominant current of energy keeping the relationship healthy and passionate.

If we let other currencies, like money, become the key focus of the relationship, it can be become far less real and nourishing to our souls. External material factors like money are poor surrogates for the one thing that romantic connections thrive upon, and that is the ever-expanding presence of love.

When we block love from inspiring our own lives and our core relationships, we will find that all becomes less natural, and we can attach to the depths of our physical illusions and needs.

Whereas if we operate within the diamond between dimensions and allow love to make our lives great, this can give us the true currency that our relationships desire: love.

CHAPTER 11

Karmic Lessons of Love

Loving Your Karma Away

If you are not open to advanced metaphysical concepts such as karmic lessons, then this chapter may not resonate with you.

However, the content in this chapter was taught to me by higher beings in channel sessions, so I put it forward as universal truths for readers to consider.

Karma is real and serves a deep purpose for our incarnations on Earth. Our karma is an Earth-bound energy that has been accumulated from this and our other lives on this planet. Our souls want us to clear our karma so that we can return to our state of pure love and become our true selves.

But this is easier said than done, particularly if we don't believe in karma or understand how it works. The age of karma is coming to an end on this planet, for those who seek to take responsibility for theirs.

The energies on this planet are now at a higher frequency than they have been for centuries, and the intelligence in this light is allowing for karma to be cleared without mirroring events needing to take place in the 3D.

For centuries, individuals have needed to experience opposing forces and events for karma to be reversed. For example, people who killed another person needed to be killed to reverse their karma.

But karma can now be cleared through self-awareness and intent.

To assist with this, there are high vibrational people and spirits who can see our past lives in the akashic records and help us to remove the energies associated with them if we choose to avail ourselves of this gift.

I have worked with a number of these amazing souls to clear the imprints of these energies in my energy field.

Our souls know what aspects of our karma they seek to clear in our current incarnations, so knowing your soul's past is crucial. After all, it was most likely other incarnations of our souls that created our karma in the first place, not the personalities that we are now living as today.

Our minds can also assist in clearing our karma in this life, should you choose to do this work, as our life circumstances can provide synchronicities that bring forth the negative energies reflective of the key karma wanting to be cleared.

Depending on your 'past' experiences on this planet, your karma can be significant or quite minimal. This differs for all of us.

Please note that I put the word 'past' in inverted commas because truly there is no such thing as a past life. All our lives are happening at once in different dimensions, as incredulous as this sounds. Therefore, any karmic energies that you clear will also flow through your soul's other concurrent lives.

Your soul, through the power of love, will then bring forth the necessary opportunities you need to cleanse your karma. Unless you want to speed up this process, like my soul drove me to do, you can simply attend to the karma that is brought forth naturally. Your soul knows how you were intended to advance in this life, so trusting this deeper aspect of yourself is critical.

Often the souls that took part in the original events that created the karma will return and become present in this life in a 3D sense, giving both souls the opportunity to restate the karmic energy.

I remember once having a significant interaction with a woman wherein, the instant that I met her, I felt major energy shifts within my form, including kundalini activations. Over a series of months, different events occurred that allowed me to confront major karma that I was impacted by energetically and discovered that she was a soul mate.

When I did karmic clearing work with the experts in this field, the spirit of this woman was then understandably relevant to a high number of them, though I never told her about this. The process gave my soul the opportunity to clear the karma that arose, and that was all that mattered.

The woman in question still does not know what took place, though her soul was present in the processes and her wholeness received the benefits of the work that was done.

Other people I know have also featured in my clearings, but not as many times as this woman.

The process of facing and clearing your karma is fascinating but can also be physically demanding, because as you process the energy releases, your body is often involved in the clearing as well.

I often experienced fatigue for a few days and cellular releases by my body.

As I progressed along my karmic clearing path, I eventually learned how to alchemise karmic energies back into the universe instantly, using advanced transmutation practices.

This has made the process faster and less physically confronting because my body is no longer doing the bulk of the processes. My soul is.

When you reach such a point in your journey, where you are embodying higher vibrations of love within your being, this transmutation process becomes possible. However, it took me 10 years of deep inner work to reach this evolutionary point, and that may not interest some readers.

Karma Doesn't Let Go Until it Can

Imagine yourself in a relationship that has lots of ups and downs, but for some reason you keep coming back together repeatedly. You feel at home in the relationship, though not fully at peace. You miss the person when you are separated, but feel tension in their presence.

Separation and reunification are very much at play here, and confusion can be felt by one or more parties. This phenomenon can be caused by karma. Essentially, the two souls in the relationship have agreed to give each other the opportunity to clear specific limiting beliefs or energies for each other, and so you are brought together, sometimes multiple times.

Once the intended lessons are learned, the two souls can either become more united or separate permanently.

I had this experience in a couple of relationships. In one we got back together three times, and in the other one we had about six separations. It's like we were joined by invisible chains that were hard to break. The magnetism was so powerful, and hard to resist.

If one or both souls separate physically without learning what was intended, the universe may simply arrange another relationship or experience for them, to give them another chance to clear their respective elements of karma. This can be with other partners or the same one. The failure to consciously learn our appropriate lessons through conscious self-reflection and truthful conversations, can cause relationships to experience these kinds of contradictory emotions, and ups and downs.

Karma won't give up on you, not even if you give up on yourself. Karma has eternity to do its loving work. It is not the curriculum, but our teacher, lifetime after lifetime. So it keeps coming for you and through you, until you face it head-on. It must be rebalanced through either deed, or awareness.

Ultimately, what you think in life helps, but energy will always override thought. You mind is no match for karmic forces and your resistance to them, rather than surrender, can be the source of much pain and suffering.

Indeed, our ignorance of this reality is the source of much heartache.

Ascension

If you clear sufficient karma to lift your vibration out of the normal 3D reality, you can enter a process often referred to as ascension.

You do not have to die to ascend, as religion has portrayed for centuries. It is available to anyone who lifts their vibration sufficiently by dissolving their egos.

If you become your multidimensional self, you will start to feel higher vibrational energies in your form.

I call this my buzz, and I discuss it farther in my book, *From Pain to Possibility*.

When this occurs, you are returning to your soul's true frequency, at which it vibrates at once it is substantially clear of its Earth-bound karma.

Some people can go through significant energetic and physical shifts during this ascension process.

Mine involved shaking and physical pressures at the base of my skull for over a year, as karmic energies left by field, body and mind.

These symptoms vary by person depending on how much karma is needing to be cleared, and the heights of the natural frequency to which your soul seeks to return.

They are orchestrated by your soul when you are deemed to be ready. The mind cannot initiate or control these releases for the mind is not consciousness, and never can be.

The ascension process often coincides with a reunion with your twin flame. This makes sense in that you are the same soul in different bodies. The soul ascends on the Earth when both halves of itself are in full and partial union, by virtue of sharing the same pure frequency of love.

Meeting your twin flame or a high-level soul mate can trigger you both to go to a higher vibration by activating your kundalini energies and challenging your core remaining wounds.

If both flames are already burning bright in their full energy of light this activation process may not even be needed!

Sexual expression with a twin flame, when both are in the energy of true love, is supposed to be a very powerful experience capable of triggering the full ascension of both souls, for in this state of union their energies connect in their fullness through their chakra systems. It's like a bomb going off inside you, so I am told (though am yet to experience for myself), as you ascend together.

The ying meets the yang with a bang.

Reconnecting With Universal Love

As a person enters a higher plane of self-love, our connection to the metaphysical realms (i.e. the As Above) can start to open.

I describe my experiences with this in detail in my book, *From Pain to Possibility*.

When we believe in the concept of separation on Earth, we close our connection to our Galactic roots. But we have in fact all lived other parts of our eternal existences in other dimensions and places in the universe.

My most recent one was Sirius.

Many of the beings in these other dimensional 'places' love us unconditionally, for this is their way of being. They are aware of their full presence in light and love.

I have had multiple conversations and interactions with my families in Sirius and other parts of the universe, and the love that they have offered me is beautiful.

Humanity fears what lies beyond our planet, yet is fascinated by what could be. We are constantly referring to the opportunity for contact to be made with 'aliens'. Ironically, we are aliens too, having a temporary experience on Earth, though we refuse to accept this truth. We are all the same stream of consciousness and universal intelligence in this great universe.

Of course, contact with other galactic beings is already possible when you access your own soul and ask them to assist you. They will and always do, for the love they have for us is immense.

One day we will collectively accept and open to this truth.

Ancestorial Karma

Each time we are born we can enter different ancestorial lines. For example, in this life you may be part of an American family and in the next life you may be French. If you've lived hundreds of times, imagine how many souls you may have interacted with, and how many families you may have belonged to.

Sometimes these families can have karmic energies that are passed down from generation to generation in their DNA and in their conditioned mindsets.

I had several experiences of clearing karma for my soul, which also assisted the karmic energies of my ancestors.

My soul did this out of love for all the souls involved.

Karmic and Soul Contracts Matter

In a metaphysical sense, many of our relationships are predetermined before we arrive on this planet. Although we have free will and can try to avoid them if we choose to, the consequences of many of our more significant relationships are governed by fate for our benefit.

In this regard there are two types of contracts worthy of note:

- Karmic contracts – in which two or more souls agree to interact in a shared incarnation with the primary purpose of releasing karmic energies from one or both of their Earth-bound energy fields.

- Soul contracts – in which two souls agree to provide loving energies to each other in their respective incarnations. This doesn't mean that they won't mirror each other to allow for personal growth to occur, through the release of limiting beliefs, but they do so with a view to establishing a loving relationship with each other. Soul contracts are normally (but not always) entered into with a twin flame or a soul mate.

Karmic contracts tend to be more challenging than soul contracts and are more likely to cause relationships to end badly than soul contracts, because their primary purpose is to stimulate pain in the interests of bringing forth higher conscious awareness.

Soul contracts are more likely to result in periods of great joy and love for both partners because that is their primary intent. They are typically based on higher vibrational matches.

How can you tell if you are in a relationship that is based on a karmic or soul contract?

It's very hard to establish this, unless you are highly psychically aware, and perhaps it doesn't matter. However, the level of the love being experienced is the key giveaway.

Soul contracts normally provide for a higher purity of love than karmic contracts and are therefore more likely to result in enduring and passionate relationships.

When you meet a soul mate or twin flame, you are likely to feel a high degree of familiarity with the other soul, because both souls remember each other from previous (or more precisely, concurrent) experiences together. They can also be full of peace depending on the circumstances.

Karmic contracts are likely to unfold at a lower frequency of love and may even be primarily ego-based experiences. They can be harsh experiences.

As such, karmic relationships are more likely to be painful and, once seen, exiting such relationships as soon as lessons have been learned is likely to be the best thing for the self-esteem of the two individuals involved.

The process of clearing karma is essentially done when you confront your limiting beliefs, but you can advance it with psychic assistance.

This level of commitment to karmic clearing, however, is not for everyone.

External Metaphysical Energies

This area is quite advanced. There are external metaphysical energies that can affect our ability to love our lives. The universe is full of many energies, and some visit our 3D realm. Some are here with positive intentions and some are not.

We have seen movies about psychic possessions and spiritual presences. Many of these are true.

I have had many experiences with negative metaphysical energies in my life, particularly after my psychic abilities opened.

I have been fortunate that I have had access to highly evolved people and beings, who have assisted me with the clearing of these energies when they have disturbed my life.

More recently I have learned to clear my own issues.

We all have energy fields around us and chakras that are susceptible to these external energies.

Astral energies, ghosts, deities, and others can attach themselves to us or enter our energy fields, infusing negative energies within our forms.

Most people are oblivious to the presence of these energies, but they can cause us to feel negative about ourselves and life. This can unknowingly impact upon our sense of self-love and self-worth, and in turn our relationships.

Love can overcome these forces of darkness, but many people are not conscious enough to resist what is taking place.

It is not unusual for me to need to clear a few astra energies from my being each month. Some can be quite discombobulating.

Our negative thoughts and energies can in fact provide a haven for their presence at times.

A strong connection to our souls, and a high sense of self-love, is our best defence against these types of negative energies.

Many spiritual people are in sync with this knowing and can assist.

PART E

CONCLUDING THIS JOURNEY INTO LOVE

CHAPTER 12

Balancing Advice for Masculine and Feminine Counterparts

Helping You Love

Earlier in this book I encouraged readers to balance out any extremes of masculine and feminine energies that they may currently have, if they wanted to open themselves up to a wider range of romantic relationship experiences.

To this aim, I offer the following broad areas of advice, aimed at increasing your individual frequency to a higher level and thus the scope of frequencies that you can and will attract.

For those who identify as having mainly masculine energies:

1. Learn to Connect to Your Feelings

Being in touch with your feelings can directly service those with predominantly more masculine energies. Not only can it offer you a new way of connecting with others, but it can increase your ability to consciously relate with your partner. In the absence of being able to offer this type of connection to your partner, they may also seek emotional expression outside of your romantic relationship, which could ultimately cause your relationship to end.

2. You are Not Just a Source of Money

Although masculine energies can very helpfully focus a person on competitiveness, protection and individual success, money is not love and never can be. This conditioned thinking is gradually diminishing, but for some people this type of thinking still pervades their subconscious beliefs. Ultimately, we enter relationships for love. Those with more feminine energies may be drawn to your ability to provide financial stability, but they generally need emotional connection to remain in love with you. They are ultimately with you for love, not money. So, love them!

3. Drop the 'Keep-Them-Happy' Mindset

This can often be the mindset of those with goal-orientated and impatient masculine energies, wherein acquiescing to their partner's apparent happiness can feel like a quicker route to their own happiness. However, there is no such thing as a quick fix when it comes to relationships, and as the chapter on conscious relating explains, your ultimate happiness in any relationship is dependent on consciously relating your experiences to your loved one. The thought that your partner's happiness will determine yours is a complete fallacy. You matter just as much as them. So drop the 'keep-them-happy' mindset, and adopt a more patient and empathetic approach to developing your long-term connection with your partner.

For those who identify as having mainly feminine energies:

1. Learn to Regulate to Your Feelings

As a person who has mainly feminine energies, you will be naturally intuitive and able to express your emotions. But try not to let those emotions dominate your relationship. It is important to go inward and discover what your feelings are telling you before you go outward and express them to others. If not, they can be unfiltered by truth. Once you have used conscious relating to communicate your perspective within a relationship, you can then employ your understanding of connectivity to prioritise your connection with your partner and the growth of your relationship. Own your emotions, don't let them own you.

2. You are Not Just a Source of Nurturing
As well as being a natural nurturer, you are your own individual self who has decided to embark on an Earth-bound existence for a purpose. That purpose may involve nurturing, which is why your form was created with mainly feminine energies. However, there might be an additional purpose to the life you are currently living, and you can seek awareness of that purpose if you choose to do so. By developing the more masculine energies of being goal-orientated, independent and focussed on individual success, you can explore the full scope of your current life and what your soul truly desires, ultimately attracting energies into your life that you need.

3. Drop the 'Keep-Them-Happy' Mindset
This can also be the mindset of those with compassionate and forgiving feminine energies, wherein acquiescing to their partner's apparent happiness can feel like a more empathetic approach, especially to conflict resolution. However, as the chapter on conscious relating explains, if both partners don't consciously relate their experiences and desires to their loved one, it can limit the relationship. So drop the 'keep-them-happy' mindset, and adopt a more independent approach to relationships that only work if you acquiesce.

CHAPTER 13

Remembering Love's Truths

Love's Key Qualities

As this book demonstrates, love is so much more than we give it credit for in our society. It is nothing, but it is also everything at the same time. Love is our greatest desire, yet mastering it is incredibly challenging for most.

But the great news is you can master it and have wonderful relationships fill your life with joy.

Here is a recap on some of the most important points that this book reveals about love:

- All too often we *think* love. This is our biggest mistake for love can never be thought. We can only love by feeling for it, through our bodies and open hearts.

- We are all pure love at our core, vibrating at various frequencies.

- Love is hard to describe in any words other than the word that appears hundreds of times in this book. Even the word 'love' does not do the feeling of love justice.

- Attraction and love are completely different. Attraction is created by mental and physical constructs. Love is non-physical only. You may love someone, but not be attracted to them, and vice versa. Nirvana is having both experiences at once at a high level on both fronts. Confusing love and attraction is a challenge for all would-be lovers.

- Love cannot be controlled or owned by the human mind. Love just is present, or isn't. Your soul will determine who you can deeply love, not your mind.

- Learning to forgive yourself and others for loving relationships that ended is a critical part of learning from these important experiences in your life and experiencing even better relationships in the future.

- Falling in love is not created by doing things together – that merely confirms whether you are compatible and sexually compatible. Simply being in each other's presence will tell you if love is present, for your presence is love. But you must be present with another to discover your love for each other. So put away those mobile phones!

- You can never be loved by another at a frequency level beyond your own frequency or threshold of self-love. Your level of self-love therefore determines the purity of love that you can attract into your life. So, increasing your own self-love is the only way to the ultimate and passionate relationships you probably desire.

- Love is a frequency or vibration. When you 'fall in love' a frequency match has become known to you. It was always present in the ether, you just became aware of it.

- Love is always pure and true. However, its frequency can be distorted by our own mental egos and energetic densities.

- Love exists between all souls, not just the ones with whom we have an intense frequency match. Our egoic minds create barriers to this reality and distort the truth of love.

- The purity of love between two souls is limited by the level of need and egoic distortions that exist between both individuals. Remove these ego-centric distortions and love can't help but grow between two people.

- The highest frequency of love between two souls is known as true love. This technically only comes into reality when both souls are in their own complete self-love, with no ego-centric forces to limit its power. True love is sometimes referred to as unconditional love because the egos of both individuals have been dissolved and conditioned beliefs and energies are not distorting the love that is present.

- All relationships are an experiment designed to help us find higher levels of consciousness and joy. Many therefore involve painful experiences, for they are helping us to expand our self-awareness and self-love.

- Few relationships are designed to be forever. Souls always come together, give each other the experiences that they are meant to, then move on, lifetime after lifetime. Expecting all romantic relationships to last forever is an unnatural expectation.

- Twin flame unions are the ultimate relationship and do last for eternity, for both souls are in fact the same soul incarnated in different forms. They are connected and remember each other forever. Twin flame reunions are very rare.

- The modern version of soul mate relationships is a myth and actually refers to a twin flame reunion. We have many soul mates with whom we journey through our lives, not just one. However, soul-based connections can be extremely loving and serene.

- Separation is used by love to provide us with opportunities to learn and grow. As our frequencies change, our souls may need us to take on new experiences for further growth. In a sense, past or present relationships can be stepping stones to the ones we now need. We therefore need to let the previous ones go so we can welcome in new intended loves and joyous learning opportunities. This can be easier said than done.

- Conscious relating can bring the force of love into our romantic relationships and allow them to be longer lasting. This is because, as we grow our self-awareness in a relationship, we are giving our souls the expanded consciousness that they seek, without needing to create a new loving relationship.

- We are all pure love at our core and give off a unique frequency. Those souls who are supposed to journey with us feel it and hear it from anywhere on the planet. When we physically come together in the 3D, our souls recognise the frequency that was already detected in the ether.

- Love is the source of everything, for the whole universe was created through the energy of love. Love, light and consciousness are all grounded in each other, for all are related to universal intelligence.

- Those who need nothing get everything, for love is no thing and it is the source of everything. Once you realise that you have everything, because you have pure self-love, you need nothing else to be happy.

- When our egos are diminished through higher self-awareness we move more into soul energy. This is where higher purity levels are possible in love.

- Love is limitless in its ability to create, for it is connected to the infinite field of intelligence of the universe. As such, so are you, through your heart.

- Love lives on after you die, for it is eternal. This is why it can still be felt with deceased souls.

- Love never dies, but attraction does. The frequency of love within us can change as we grow in awareness, diminishing our love match with another soul.

- The combination of high frequency love and powerful attraction allows for what we all tend to seek, and refer to as true love.

- The primary love relationships in your life are intended by souls and will be given the opportunity to manifest into your life. The feeling of love will be unmistakable when these events take place. However, the Earth is a place of free will, so you can avoid them if that is your mind's preference. Be careful though, because resistance can generate pain within you.

- Karmic and soul-based contracts entered into before your birth govern the nature of these intended relationships. Karmic contracts normally bring forth significant learnings as their key intention, they can be painful and ruthless. Soul-based contracts will often do the same but will also bring forth love and immense joy for both parties to enjoy.

- When we grow our vibrational pitch, the universe will normally give us a love at a higher frequency next time. This is its way of advancing us all to loving relationships of increasing purity.

- Karmic energies from past lives can, and often do, impact the energies we carry in this life, into the relationship with ourselves and others. These can be cleared, but that takes higher awareness to address.

CHAPTER 14

My Ode to Love

My Verse for this Universe

I am not a recognised poet, but I feel called to feel into and express my greatest sense of appreciation for love.

Love's wisdom took on my lack of self-awareness and prevailed. Love gave me what I needed, which often came with great pain and discomfort, but it was always there, holding me in its tender embrace. It saw me through it all, such was its never-ending care and compassion.

And in the end, to get what I desired, all I had to do was surrender and trust in my heart. For only it knew who and what I really was.

"Love was in my everywhere,
and in my everything;
It was in my cold of winter,
and in my sense of spring;
I breathed it in the mountain air,
and swam with it at sea;
All the while oblivious
To what it truly meant to me.

It never wore a mask, you see, but hid in open view,
Aware that I had blinkers on to what was always true.

I saw it in my good times,
And wanted it to stay;
But it had a plan for everything
And always knew the way.

Crashed upon the rocks
And smashed upon the sea,
Its endless waves of wisdom
Finally led me home to me.

Now I recognise its face again
in everything I know;
It holds me in its loving arms
And will never let me go.
I'll never try to separate
from the vibration that is love,
For now I know that it's divine
and always comes from up above.

It had a bigger plan for me
and waited so patiently,
Until I could trust its every move
And take me forth with thee.
Now I've walked up the steps of love,
Sometimes all alone;
And seek only your loving arms
For there, we'll both be home."

I dedicate this poem to a world that unknowingly craves what it already has in infinite abundance: love.

CHAPTER 15

Knowing Thyself as Pure Love

You Are the Love That You Seek

We all think we know how to love. So did I when I journeyed forth as an adult, only to experience my share of painful separations. This bewildered me, given I applied everything the world had shown me growing up with strong levels of commitment.

But how can we become the masters of something we do not understand? We can't!

This book can, however, give you the upper hand in love, and the wisdom to come into greater alignment with the love that you desire. Love is the main thing we all seek in our lives. We all want to be loved and to love. We are constantly engaged in activities to prove that we are lovable and avoid others who may confirm the fact that we are not.

Love is our natural state of being and reflects the truth that we are all connected through universal energies, including love and light.

While we may seek love and intimacy from others, we are often unaware that the most reliable and purest of loves is available within our own hearts. Our own self love is the most powerful and reliable love of all, and it determines the purity of love that you can share with another. It is where our love endeavours are highly valuable.

We may often feel a hole in our heart, because our ego can create shadows across it with its limiting and conditioned beliefs. The truth is that our hearts are whole and always were. They give us the experiences we need to become fully aware of this reality.

A heart truly never breaks. It is just trying to break free from the clutches of our illusions that tell us that we are not worthy of love. By giving us the pain we attribute to a breaking heart, it is challenging us to go inward and find deeper consciousness within ourselves, which will lead us to recognise ourselves as the love that we are.

For centuries, our ignorance about love has kept us in a dark place. This has extended itself on a grand scale in countless forms of relationships, even between societies and nations. Loving relationships have become battlefields for blame and despair, as we naïvely try to cope with separations that were actually designed to lift our conscious awareness. We have become blinded to the big truth that will soften the blows of such separation. Put simply: we do not understand love's intent and ignorantly put it in a box called failure.

The journey home to true self-love is found in and sparked by the repeated cycle of separation, back to union. Until we learn to conquer this painful cycle, it will continue to burden us with its regularity and ruthlessness.

We need to be able to connect to our own hearts and let them lead us through life. This will allow us to expand through the application of self-awareness to all our relationships.

Love is always giving us what we need, before it gives us what we want. This is the pathway we must walk upon this planet, until we don't. We can take this pathway to knowing ourselves as love in either a state of ignorance or intelligence.

Either way, you are the love you seek from others, and you always were. It is time to remind our minds that we are worthy of love, no matter what happens in our lives. It's time we forgave ourselves for love's lost, and get excited about what is possible for us all in love. It is truly infinite and beyond our wildest dreams. There is so much hope that can arise from loving your way through different relationships and enjoying the beautiful experiences and colours that they can bring to your life!

Higher awareness allows you to make choices from a higher intelligence level in your life, and love is the key to doing this. You can take your life to a whole new level when you embrace what the energy of love can teach you.

We all deserve to have romantic relationships that are based on the passion and purity of love. We deserve mutual love where both partners are together for each other, with each other and as each one; together in presence, with beautiful intimacy and mutual respect.

That's my dream for all my readers!

Love is not matter, but it is all that truly matters in our journey to higher conscious awareness. We are here to evolve back to self-love, and from there to love life, being one with our true selves. This means trusting the love within you, for it knows what is in your best interests, always.

Although this goes against all that we have been taught, your heart now wants you to know the truth. We have all suffered far too much and greater joy awaits.

In Michael Jackson's wonderful song 'Heal the World', he asks us to make this world a better place by living more from love, caring more for each other, allowing us all to live again and shine in grace. I fully support this adventure, and it all starts by realising that this world can be heavenly, if we become fully aware of what we already are, and that is pure love.

There is an endless stream of love in this world. It is everywhere and ever-present. We just don't believe it, yet. But it's time we did.

It is not a race, but seeing the journey home to your heart with clarity and gratitude, and not confusion, is the fastest way to the frequency of love that we all seek.

It took me ten years to unravel our collective confusion about love. I offer this book to help turn your confusion into clarity, changing your world in the process.

It's time we healed this world with the only power that can really do it, love!

Acknowledgements

I would like to thank you, the reader, for spending your valuable time reading this book. I consider it a great privilege to share my learnings and discoveries with people on a similar journey into higher awareness.

I acknowledge the beautiful souls who have interacted with me in this life and held their magic mirrors up for me to see myself more clearly within. They have helped to make this book possible.

I am particularly grateful to the women who have shared romantic relationships with me during my life. They were all incredible women, and they helped me to grow immensely. I am sorry if I caused any of them undue pain.

In terms of the production of this book, I wish to thank Zena Shapter for again bringing greater light and clarity to my words. This is the fourth book she has helped me to create with her wonderful editing skills and sharp mind.

Her husband, Bill Shapter, provided his graphic artistry to the diagrams and pictures in this book to help it come to life for readers.

I love your work, Shapters!

Julia Kuris designed the covers for the book, and her creative genius has again brought this important book to life. She is blessed in her creative abilities.

Andrea Gussy provided her wonderful proofreading abilities to help complete this labour of love. She is an intelligent lady and has an amazing eye for detail.

Again, I thank my wonderful children for always encouraging me on my journey to my own truths. I love them dearly, and they continue to teach me much about life in their own beautiful ways.

About the Author

Mark discovered the concepts embodied in this book after his love life was punctuated with repeated doses of separation. He tried extremely hard to make relationships work for much of his life, with limited success.

This led him to undertake deep enquiries into the important topic of love. He consulted far and wide, including holding discussions with some very learned human and metaphysical mentors to get a better understanding of this powerful energy.

Aligning love with conscious awareness was a huge breakthrough that led him to begin to foster deeper understandings of love. He then did extensive inner-work to dispel his own illusions around love.

Facing the disappointments of his love life with pure integrity and a passion for learning, has allowed him to unearth deep wisdom about love, which he now shares in this book with readers.

Mark is an expert in love and consciousness and has written four ground-breaking books on how a person can attain higher levels of self-love, then apply it to important areas of their life, including relationships, living a happier life, becoming a more conscious leader, resolving pain and completing spiritual journeys back to universal love and intelligence.

His greatest wish is to help others to take their lives to a whole new level through higher awareness of the power of love. In this totally natural state, we can make better choices in our lives, and live a more beautiful life full of love.

Is there any more important area to understand the truth of than love?

Mark lives in Sydney, Australia, and has five wonderful children.

Should you wish to discuss any part of this book in greater depth, Mark can be reached through his website at mark-worthington.com, or by email at mark@mark-worthington.com

www.ingramcontent.com/pod-product-compliance
Lightning Source LLC
Chambersburg PA
CBHW072010070526
44583CB00015B/1418